blue

NICK PAGE

blue

HarperCollins*Publishers*

HarperCollins*Publishers*
77–85 Fulham Palace Road, London W6 8JB
www.**fire**and**water**.com

First published in Great Britain in 2001 by
HarperCollins*Publishers*

10 9 8 7 6 5 4 3 2 1

Copyright © 2001 Nick Page

Nick Page asserts the moral right to be
identified as the author of this work

A catalogue record for this book is
available from the British Library

ISBN 0 551 03265 0

Printed and bound in Great Britain by
Martins the Printers, Berwick upon Tweed

blue

There was once a man who wanted to fly in a balloon. That was his dream and his ambition: to rise above the earth; to rise into the blue sky and leave the world behind him...

■ ■ ■ ■

Many periods have a colour.

The decadent 1890s were known as the 'mauve decade'; the sun-kissed, hedonistic, youthful 1920s were the 'golden twenties'. We have lived through the 'grey' fifties, drab with rationing and the effects of a devastating war, a period which was followed by the swirling, multicoloured, psychedelic sixties.

For many people, the 1990s were the 'green' decade, a time when we discovered renewable energy, recycling bins, sustainable forestry and organic vegetables. Worried about the state of the planet, concerned about the future, fearful of what humankind is doing in the world, we spent the nineties trying to figure out how to save our planet.

One look at society is enough to show that, good as they are, green values have done little to change the world. The environmental problems loom as large as they have ever done, but, more importantly, a decade of going green has solved none of the underlying problems. 'Green' values told us how to create a sustainable environment, but not how to sustain our relationships; they showed us how to recycle our tin cans, but not how to renew our lives; they encouraged us to be friends of the earth, but somewhere along the way we forgot how to be friends with each other.

Perhaps it is time we looked at a different colour. Perhaps it is time we raised our eyes from the green earth and started to look into the blue.

■ ■ ■ ■

When I go into my supermarket now I see a huge display of organic vegetables. Ten years ago, organic produce was available to only a handful of devotees, but now I can easily buy meat, fruit, washing powders and even toilet paper.

It is an example of how the green values – once seen as the province of hippies and eccentrics – have gradually become mainstream. We no longer question their wisdom. We expect our local government to have 'green' policies. Every village has its bottle bank, every street its paper recycling collection. In the course of the 1990s the green values have moved out from the garden and into the high street.

All of this is good. I do not want to attack green values, many of which I agree with. The problem with green values, however, is not what they give us but what they do not give us – indeed, what they alone can never give us.

For much of the 1990s the impression was given that all we had to do to save the planet was to 'go green'. The green values were presented to us as though they were some kind of universal solution, the only way forward for all humankind. In some respects this is correct. We cannot go on wasting the earth's resources indefinitely. We cannot be profligate with energy and nonrenewable resources. We cannot keep filling the world with chemicals and pollutants and not expect it to have some kind of effect.

But the real problem lies deeper. It lies in the kind of desires and attitudes which got the world into this mess in the first place. To these the green values have no real answer. Selfishness, greed, arrogance, loneliness, isolation, despair – all these pollute the planet as surely as CFCs and diesel fumes. Yes, there is a hole in the ozone layer, but there is a greater hole in society, a massive chasm which the green values alone cannot satisfy. The green values sought to change our behaviour, but they could do little to change our hearts.

For this reason, our adoption of green values remains largely superficial. There are more cars on the road now than there were in 1990. We use more power, not less. We put our cans and bottles in the recycling bin, we buy organic carrots, we start making compost in the garden, but inside we have not really changed. We are still profligate with energy, addicted to overconsumption, secretly slipping out to indulge in our very unorganic burgers and chips. We use unleaded fuel, true – but we use it to fill huge, gas-guzzling four-wheel-drive vehicles that deliver about three yards to the gallon.

Why is this? If the green values were so compelling, why have they still had such a superficial impact?

The answer lies in the presence of another colour, a much more powerful shade, hidden below the thin coat of green paint – another set of values that was every bit as much a part of the 1990s and which is far more of a threat to the world than carbon dioxide emissions will ever be.

■ ■ ■ ■

For all its success in the 1990s, green was not the only colour. There was another pigment there – a bright, brassy colour, glinting in the sunlight with the promise of gold. It was not gold. It was fake. It was gilt.

This was the era, above all others, of mass consumerism and mass consumption. It was the era when we all became customers, consumers, valued not for who we were, but for what we could spend.

It was the era when money not only talked, it shouted, screamed and yelled. It was a time when currency speculators walked the earth, when we all bowed down at the shrine of wealth, when happiness and fulfilment were promised through the latest car, computer or cosmetic surgery. Shopping became retail therapy and the internet – which was created to be a global community – was taken over by pornographers and speculators. (When I was first on the internet, in the early 1990s, the buzz word was 'community'; at the end of the decade everyone was talking about 'e-commerce'.)

Everything was reduced to a saleable commodity. Political policies were decided on the basis of what the public would 'buy' with their votes. In the end, even the green values were subverted – the German Green Party dropped their plans for a petrol tax when it became clear that it was going to be a vote-loser.

■ ■ ■ ■

The green values could not provide happiness and satisfaction, but the gilt values did not even try. Oh, they promised it, certainly, but their ultimate aim was to keep us as customers, which means that we must remain perpetually dissatisfied.

It is not in the interest of big businesses to have happy, contented people, for happy, contented people are less in need of cigarettes, alcohol, drugs, plastic surgery, fashion items, diet plans, get-rich-quick books, the National Lottery, therapy and divorce lawyers.

We never noticed this. We thought that their way was the best way, and we got sucked in. The green values, for all their strength, could not compete with the bright and shiny gilt.

The gilt values, however, have failed completely. Society has got worse, not better. In Britain in 1950 some 6,000 crimes of violence were reported to the police. In 1996 that figure had risen to 239,000. Rates of depression have grown, as have rates of suicide. Homeless numbers have risen, divorce rates have skyrocketed, drug abuse is endemic, alcoholism rife.

These are extremes, it is true, but at a lower level, the failure of the gilt values is apparent. Everywhere I see tired, unhappy people. Each year, thousands of people take sick leave because of 'stress'. For all our affluence, for all our technological advances, we are a fragmented society, full of loneliness, anger and fear. The streets are full of people who know that there is a better life out there somewhere, but who are so tied into the gilt values that they cannot see beyond the cheap gold that glitters in their eyes.

■ ■ ■ ■

Thus the real story of the 1990s was the story of the battle between the green and the gilt, between global capitalism and global renewal.

Green values tell us to look outwards, but gilt values tell us that the only thing that matters is 'me'. Our sense of responsibility and self-preservation makes us adopt green values, but it is like putting a thin coat of paint on a mirror. The slightest scratch reveals the true, shiny, self-centred surface underneath.

You cannot build a green society on gilt values. They are fundamentally opposed. The essence of a green economy is responsibility, awareness of others and the environment, sacrificing our own ease for the good of others. The essence of the gilt society is exactly the opposite: putting myself first, every man or woman for themselves. Let others save the rainforest, I need a new coffee table. The green movement might save the whale, but in the gilt movement it's dog eat dog.

The presence of the gilt values in our lives means that, at best, the green values will only be superficial. What we need is a new set of values. We need something more basic than green, something which will drive out the gilt and give us real answers to the questions that plague our lives. We need a primary colour. We need to look into the blue.

■ ■ ■ ■

Seen from space, the earth is blue.
Yuri Gagarin, the first man in space

■ ■ ■ ■

At a conference in 1999, two American futurologists declared that the colour of the millennium is blue. They were pointing out a global phenomenon – the upsurge of interest in spirituality and religion. People are looking outwards and upwards, searching for answers to the really important questions, believing that the truth, to coin a phrase, is out there. There is an interest in issues that are deeper than the surface, issues that are not just about *how* we behave – whether we recycle energy, preserve the environment, save the whale – but *why* we should behave in that way.

■ ■ ■ ■

If we doubt that people are looking at more 'spiritual' matters, we only have to look at the numbers of people going on pilgrimage.

Pilgrimage is popular again. A decade ago less than 4,000 people made the trek along Spain's pilgrim route to Santiago. In the summer of 1996, 95,000 undertook the journey. Why? Because people are on the move. Or, more precisely, their hearts are on the move. Gradually, the restlessness transmits itself to all parts of their bodies, until they cannot help but start walking.

The 1990s saw more and more people turn their back on the gilt-valued rat race and pursue alternative lifestyles. Dissatisfied with the life around them, they are doing whatever it takes to find the answers.

Sometimes, admittedly, this quest takes strange routes. There has been a massive surge of interest in 'alternative' religions. Bookshops, the internet and magazines are full of weird ideas which are often little more than traps for the credulous. Nonetheless, it is interesting that people are searching. They might be looking in the wrong place, but at least they are looking. The pupil who gets the sum wrong is at least attempting to do the arithmetic.

People are on the move. They are questing for the truth. They are dissatisfied with what they have been given, suspicious of what they have been told. Weary of cynicism and lies, painfully aware that 'there must be more to life than this', they have packed their bags and started on the pilgrimage.

■ ■ ■ ■

This book is about that journey. It is an attempt to look at some different values, some values which will give meaning to life and significance to the journey. It is not a quick-fix solution, for pilgrimages are not quick. Truth has to be discovered. It cannot be delivered like a pizza. We cannot order fulfilment over the internet, pay with our credit card and have it delivered to our door.

No. To go into the blue means starting to think for ourselves. It means taking a journey and starting to grapple with those things that need changing in our lives. It means travelling to a place of understanding, and then further – to a place of believing. It means climbing mountains, not to gain altitude but to change attitude.

The difficulty should not surprise us. 'Travel' was originally the same as the word 'travail', which comes from the French for 'work'. Travelling, at least in early times, was not easy and comfortable but hard and arduous. The kind of travelling we will have to undertake is similarly demanding. We cannot go into the blue on a day trip – at least, not if we really want our lives to change. We are travellers, not tourists; we are explorers heading into the unknown. We want to encounter the reality, not view life through the distance of the camera lens. We want to be changed by the journey, thrilled, excited, challenged, restored, fulfilled.

All books are journeys. All lives are pilgrimages.

■ ■ ■ ■

The 'blue' values are hope, faith, stillness, truth, mercy, wonder, friendship and celebration.

These are the values I think we are missing, the fertile ground in which green values can take root and which shows up the gilt values for the sham they really are. These are the values I want to explore, the journey I want to make in this book.

There is, in one sense, nothing new about these values. They are in many ways old values, just seen from new angles. That is always the way: in order to change the future we must rediscover the past.

After all, all voyages of discovery are really rediscovery. Explorers penetrating into the heart of unmapped continents found new things that were very old. They 'discovered' waterfalls and mountains, valleys and plains, all of which had been known to the natives for years. Maybe their achievement lies not in what they thought they did, but in the fact that they brought these wonders before a world ignorant of their existence. 'See!' they said. 'Look at the wonders that exist in this world. They were here all the time, and yet we never knew of them.'

■ ■ ■ ■

What is blue?
Blue is the invisible becoming visible...

Yves Klein

■ ■ ■ ■

The power of profound meaning is found in blue ...
Blue is the typical heavenly colour.

Wassily Kandinsky

■ ■ ■ ■

From *Brewer's Dictionary of Phrase and Fable*, some meanings of 'blue':

Blue: peace, harmony, a sense of adventure
Ecclesiastical use: hope, contemplation, piety, sincerity
Art: fidelity and faith, modesty, humility
Heraldry: chastity, loyalty and fidelity

Phrase and fable – these are just about the only weapons a writer has. That is why this has to be told as part journal, part story – or, if you like, two stories, two journeys.

■ ■ ■ ■

This journey, this book, is about values which will help us to change our world. They will make sense of the green and wipe out the gilt. They will point us in a new direction. They are blue values, and it is time to start the journey; time to enter the blue.

There was once a man who wanted to fly in a balloon. That was his dream and his ambition: to rise above the earth; to rise into the blue sky and leave the world behind him.

For many years, this dream possessed him. He would talk about flying, dream about flying, write about flying, wish with all his heart to fly, and yet something seemed to hold him back.

'I can't afford it,' he would say to himself. Or, 'I'm not insured.'. To take his mind off the dream which possessed him, he would fill his days with tasks or appointments. 'I'm too busy,' he would mutter to himself when the dream raised its head. And, as the years went by, he added, 'I'm too old.'

None of these reasons, of course, was the truth. The reality was that he was scared. The dream was so important to him that he did not want to risk its beauty by turning it into reality. Life had disappointed this man so many times that he had come to believe that the dream was better than the fulfilment.

So his life went by. He woke in the morning, went to his work, came home and went to bed. At the weekends he worked on his house, or tended the garden, or went for long walks during which he tried not to think about flying.

Then, one day, a letter arrived. He opened it and found inside a printed invitation.

The Big Blue Balloon Company invites you to a FREE balloon ride.

This is a once-in-a-lifetime opportunity.
Free passage. Fly into the blue with us!
All who hope will fly. Wait and we will come.

There was no phone number, no return address. Just that single phrase: 'All who hope will fly. Wait and we will come.'

At first, he thought it might be a trick, a joke played on him by his friends. The problem with this theory was that he did not have any friends – or, at least, not the type of friends who would play jokes on him. (Indeed, he sometimes wished for the type of friends who would play more tricks and liven his life up, but that was the way it was – all the laughs seemed to happen elsewhere.)

He threw it down in disgust. 'Just a circular,' he said to himself. 'I'll bet everyone in the neighbourhood got one.'

As the days went by, however, he could not get the invitation out of his mind. Although he asked his neighbours, no one else, it appeared, had received the same offer. So, despite his reservations, his mind began to ask questions. What if it were true? What if he could actually fly in a balloon? At last he would get what his heart most desired – and feared.

'I must get to the bottom of this,' he decided, so he set out to find the company responsible. His search proved full of obstacles. They were not in the phone book. None of the other ballooning companies had heard of them. For many days he looked around him.

Each day, on the way to work, he would scan the skies eagerly for signs. He read the papers, watched the TV, scoured the internet. There was no mention of the company. He spent his free time walking from park to park, from hill to hill, all the places where he knew that balloons would fly. There was no sign of the company.

Days came and went. He saw no balloons. No one called him on the phone or knocked at his door. In a moment of unfamiliar optimism he even packed a bag, ready for the trip, in case the call should come – but the bag just sat there in the hall, a glaring reminder of unrealized hopes. He tried to convince himself that the whole thing was a dream, a foolish misunderstanding. Yet something kept him hoping, because he knew, deep down, that it was what he wanted. What he desired was for someone to come and lift him from the ground, to make his dreams come true.

Then, one morning, he woke with a start. His room was filled with a curious blue light. Where sunshine should have been pouring through the windows, the room was shrouded in a coloured shadow.

It was not, however, the light which had woken him, but the noise. From the garden came a roaring, hissing sound. It sounded like a waterfall or an animal. It was the rumble of a volcano, the fire of a dragon; it was the breath of God.

He leapt from his bed, rushed to the window and threw back the curtains.

There, towering into the sky before him, was a

huge, blue hot-air balloon. It filled the horizon, a cathedral of fabric, billowing in the gentle breeze. Below it, a large wicker basket was sitting in the rose bushes. In the basket a small figure was pulling on a cord and working a large burner, sending heat into the canopy of the balloon.

The figure looked up, smiled and waved. The man opened the window.

'What?' he said. 'How ... that is ... er ... who...?'

The figure seemed to squeal with delight. 'You see?' shouted a voice. 'I told you I'd come!'

hope

Towards the end of 1999, I listened to a phone-in on the radio. It was an argument about when the millennium actually began, with some callers arguing that it began on 1 January 2000, while others said that we should all calm down as it was not due to begin until 1 January 2001. Apart from a nagging feeling that everyone involved in this debate ought to get out more, I could not help feeling that they were missing the point.

The millennium – or at least, the excitement about the millennium – was not a matter of arithmetic, but emotion. Looked at logically, mathematically even, there was no difference between 31 December 1999 and 1 January 2000. All that happened was that another 24 hours were added to the total, another digit to the number of years, another revolution of the planet.

That is not what people were excited about, however. What mattered were the noughts. The number looked different. The 'nines' were gone and it was as though we had started again.

I drive a Morris Minor (yes, it is blue – although, as it was made in 1968, I can hardly claim it to be an expression of the millennium) and I remember a few years ago when it went 'round the clock'. After reaching 99,999 miles on the mileometer, it reset itself to 00,000. Sad man that I am, I drove up and down a tiny, deserted road in Sussex, just so that I could stop easily and take a photograph of the dashboard at that crucial moment.

Why? After all, it was just another mile, and a pretty boring mile at that. It was more than that, though. This was a significant occasion. It was more than a mile: it was a milestone, a landmark. It was a reminder, in fact, that my battered old car had once been young, that once it had no miles on the clock. It was a pointer back to the beginning, when the car had all its journeys ahead of it.

■ ■ ■ ■

Here is another example. My credit card bill is in, revealing the usual sorry tale of expensive bargains and too many book purchases. How I would love it if, just once, the bill read £0.00. Zero is also the number of freedom, of no debts, no money owed.

Or think of it as a race. A race begins at 0.00 seconds on the clock. The gun fires and the sprinters leap from their blocks, their hearts full of hope that they will win.

Zero is the number of a new beginning.

Zero means that we can start again.

It was the noughts in the date that inspired a feeling of hope. They inspired in us the hope, however dimly recognized, that things might actually be different this time, that this millennium would be free from the bad things of the past.

Naturally, such optimism made some people react with cynicism. As if a change of date could change anything! But they misunderstood. The date was merely a reminder. For a moment the world remembered what it was to hope, and we had almost forgotten what that felt like…

Human beings are hoarders. We store up memories – so much so that sometimes we hardly realize they are there. Many years ago my grandfather was a watch repairer. Some years back I went into another watch repair shop and there was the same smell. Immediately I was whisked back into my grandfather's workshop, back to my childhood, with him hunched over his watches, oiling, cleaning, fixing.

The turning of the year brought a reminder of something that we thought we had lost for ever. As the years went by, we had forgotten it was there. Tricked by the cynicism and disbelief all around us, we had lost the art of hoping. We truly believed that nothing ever changes. There, however, on that millennium night, I saw signs of hope. I saw it rise again, a tiny flower pushing out of the hard earth, bravely flowering in the cold night air.

■■■■

A leaflet in my letterbox cries out, 'IS THERE HOPE FOR THE WHITE RHINO?' I don't know. I would like to think so. It is not just the poor, beleaguered rhino who needs hope, however. All around me there is a society desperate for things to change, a world of people every bit as endangered and unsure of survival.

■■■■

It is not hard to see why people want a fresh start. Look at the papers — themselves often filled with a kind of despairing cynicism — and you will see what a mess we have made of society and the world.

Many people are deeply unhappy and dissatisfied with their lives. They work all the hours they can, earn all the money they can, but it does not seem to make a difference. They yearn for peace and happiness, but have virtually given up hope of finding it.

Newspapers report that one in every seven women has felt suicidal because of the stresses of modern-day living. Among young men, the suicide rates have shot up — in Britain alone they have trebled since 1970. As the century turns and the new millennium dawns, surveys reveal that we are anywhere between three and ten times more likely to suffer from depression than our ancestors in 1900.

For so many people life appears hopeless. They

have nowhere to turn, nothing to cling to. The brave new world has turned out to be worse than the one we left behind.

■ ■ ■ ■

The mass of men lead lives of quiet desperation.
Henry David Thoreau

■ ■ ■ ■

You can see it on their faces – etched lines of despair. I once saw a polar bear in a zoo. The creature was walking up and down, up and down, its head waving from side to side. It was trapped in its cage. Something in it yearned for the wide open spaces, for the cleansing cold of its natural habitat. Instead it had concrete and iron bars. Some people have given up on escaping. Instead they pace up and down their cage, exploring their own loneliness.

■ ■ ■ ■

I remember years ago sitting with my family watching *The Poseidon Adventure* – a film about a shipwreck, a kind of poor man's *Titanic*. One character is trapped in a room, unable to move as the waters slowly rise around her. Eventually the waters reach her neck and soon she is straining with all her might to keep her face above water. I remember looking round the room as everyone watched that scene and, as one, we were all echoing her movements, all lifting our heads in an unconscious imitation of the person on the screen.

This image is not so far from the faces I saw on the streets of the city today: grim faces, stern faces, anxious faces; faces that looked for all the world as if the tide was about to roll in and sweep them away. Their life is hectic beyond belief. They are prey to constant demands. They work all the hours God gives, swimming as fast as they can but never reaching the shore. Today, it is not pride that makes us hold our heads high, but the fear of drowning.

Many people are struggling to keep their heads above water. They want their life to change, they want the pressure to ease, the hurts to go away. They are lost at sea, sending up their distress flares, hoping quietly, desperately, that someone, somewhere, will come to their aid.

■ ■ ■ ■

The way that elephant handlers train their charges in India is simple. When the elephant is very young and relatively weak, they tether one of its hind legs to a post. At first the baby elephant rebels against this and tries to pull the post away, but gradually it dawns on the creature that his strength is not enough. He cannot budge it. Eventually, he decides to give up. Now, when an elephant decides something, it *really* decides and, despite the fact that the handler never alters the size of the post, the creature never tries to escape again. Even when the elephant has grown to the size where he could easily pull up an oak tree, he remains tethered to this tiny post, because he believes that it cannot be moved. He tried it years ago, and it did not work.

Perhaps the proverb is true. Perhaps the elephant's memory is so strong that it becomes a kind of prison: because he knows what has always been, he is incapable of imagining what might be.

Most of us have posts to which we are tethered, ways of doing things that seem important, although we can no longer really remember why. We hate the captivity, resent the restrictions on our movement – but we cannot be bothered to give the chain a tug. We tried it long ago and it was no use. Now we are older, we know better. We are 'wise in the ways of the world'. We 'know' that life is tough, and that we all have to settle for second best. Metal chains are one thing; the really hard chains to break are the ones in our own heads.

Hope is the sound of the elephant tugging on the chain. Hope is the idea that maybe, just maybe, the stake is not as big as we thought. Maybe, if we pull hard enough or long enough, the earth will crumble, the chain will come loose and we will be free.

■ ■ ■ ■

In the old Greek myth about Pandora, Pandora opened a jar which she had been warned never to open. Out of the jar flew all the evils that were to plague humankind – 'old age, labour, sickness, insanity, vice and passion', as it says in my version of the legend. Last of all, when all these evils had escaped, when all the world had turned black, when nobody could see any point in going on, out fluttered a butterfly. The butterfly was hope.

Without hope, we cannot go on. Were it not for hope, we might as well climb into the jar and seal up the lid. Hope is a fragile creature, however – a rare bloom, a fluttering butterfly, an endangered species.

■ ■ ■ ■

The problem is that we generally reverse Pandora's story. Hope flutters free from the jar, but, tethered by years of disappointment, hardened by too many broken promises, too many lies, we release all the other predators after it: disillusionment, apathy, cynicism, weariness, despair – all the enemies that will hunt down hope and crush its wings.

If hope is to lead anywhere, therefore, it must be protected. We must put aside the belief that nothing can change. We must nurture people's hopes, protect and encourage them. We must not give up. If we are to preserve this most delicate of creatures, we need to throw out all those things which would destroy it.

I am constantly battling cynicism. Yet I am becoming aware that, if I am to be a hopeful person, if I am to be any kind of force for change in the world around me, I must try to see the best in people. I must try to reject my old, preconceived ideas and seek to find what is good in others, what is genuine, pure and worth discovering. That does not mean I have to be gullible and naive. Jesus, after all, famously told his followers to be as wise as serpents and as innocent as doves. However, just because there are some people who want to con me, it does not mean that everyone is up to the same tricks. If we have been let down in the past, does that mean that we will always be let down in the future?

Pandora's butterfly emerged after everything else. After all the hurts, lies, betrayals and weary sadnesses of life had flown from the jar, out crawled this tiny, fragile creature. It needs my protection and my courage.

If we are to change things now, we have to show that trusting is not always stupid, that believing is not the same as being tricked. We have to show that sometimes, when you hope for the best, that is exactly what you get.

■ ■ ■ ■

Everyone has to build anew his sky of hope and peace.
Kakuzo Okakura

■ ■ ■ ■

A man looks down at the simple bed; at his child, the embodiment of his hopes and dreams. No breath.

Nothing but her thin, pale face. A fly lands on her cheek. It walks across her face and he does not even bother to brush it away. Throughout the household he can hear the keening, the cries and wailing, women and men crying in impotent rage against heaven. He turns and puts on his cloak.

Outside it is hot and bright, but he is walking in a deep, dark valley and he has only one small, flickering flame.

The teacher is speaking when he arrives. He is talking about wine. No, he is talking about newness. It does not matter. The man walks up to the teacher and kneels. Everything in him wants to fall onto the floor and beat the dust with his hands. Everything in him wants to cry out. But he kneels. Something in him tells him he will never understand unless first he kneels.

'My daughter has just died, but come: put your hand on her and she will live.'

There is a moment when he can feel the shape of all his hopes. He could touch them. They are delicate. Brittle. The weight of one word would be enough to smash them into pieces.

No word comes. The teacher rises, gently lifts him to his feet, and together they start to walk...

Back at the house, the flute players have arrived, trilling their mournful tunes. Who could think that these dirges would ever be comforting? Or perhaps that is not the point. Perhaps their aim is to fill the air with noise so that no one will have to think about that awful silence.

'Go away!' The teacher starts to hustle the flautists out of the door. 'Go away,' he says again. 'The girl is not dead, but only sleeping.'

There is bitter laughter. Still he pushes the crowd outside. They are death and they are defiling a temple, a holy place.

Then he goes into the room where the little girl lies. The man cannot bear to follow. He has looked at death once that day and he knows he cannot be that brave again. There is no noise. Nothing at all. Nothing happens. Then a fly slowly buzzes out of the room. That is what he notices first: the fly.

He rushes to the door. The girl is sitting up, holding the teacher's hands. The man looks at his daughter and, for the first time that day, he starts to cry.

■ ■ ■ ■

There is a line in the Bible that used to worry me. It occurs in the book of Revelation, where the writer is describing heaven, painting a vivid portrait of a place where suffering and sadness no longer have a part, where the tears will be dried up. He also says, 'And the sea shall be no more.'

It is a curious phrase and, on the face of it, not an attractive one. I like the sea. I enjoy a paddle. I love building sand castles. I would like there to be a seaside in heaven.

The point, however, is not geographical but symbolic. Most ancient nations hated the sea. The sea was not something you travelled on unless you absolutely had to. Not for them a weekend's yachting on the Med. In an age when all navigation had to be done by the stars, ships kept close to the land where it was at all possible. The sea was a dark and treacherous place. At sea, people were out of their depth, with nothing below them, no solid ground and nothing to rely on.

Today we echo this feeling in the phrase 'all at sea', which speaks of someone who is lost, aimless, adrift on an ocean of confusion.

It is that feeling which the writer of Revelation says God will take away. He was looking to a time when humans will always have a solid footing – when we will never again feel as if we are drowning.

I believe that hope will be rewarded and that lives can change. If I did not believe this, then I would pack it in today. I would stop writing, thinking and arguing. After all, if nothing changes, then why bother?

Just imagine, though – imagine what it would be like if we could actually reach land, if we could actually lead fulfilled, happy lives. Imagine what it would be like if we could love and be loved, trust and be trusted. Isn't that a prize worth believing in? Isn't that a hope worth holding close to our hearts?

■ ■ ■ ■

It all begins with imagination. Every great change in society has begun when one person sat down and imagined what could be.

We must look at our lives with imagination. We must ask ourselves: What would I like my life to be like? What would make it better? What do I really want it to be?

Then ... then we must start walking. We must do all we can, dare all we can, strive with all our heart to reach that destination – that point where hope becomes reality and what we imagined comes to pass.

■ ■ ■ ■

I believe that the first of the blue values is hope. Without hope, we can achieve nothing. Without the belief that things can change, nothing will change. If we would find the true values, we must first believe that they are there to discover. Like the explorers, we must first set out on the journey.

So many people have settled for a blank, hopeless existence. 'Life isn't going to get any better,' they reason. 'I might as well just make the best of a bad job.' Thus their lives remain unaltered. They never look up into the blue sky and wonder what it would be like to fly. They merely glance at the clouds in the expectation of rain.

Robert Louis Stevenson once wrote that 'to travel hopefully is better than to arrive'. It is not true. If there were no destination, there would be no cause for hope. He is right, however, in the sense that without hope we would not even set foot out of the door.

Small events have huge consequences. Scientists talk about chaos theory – precisely the idea that small events can have huge consequences. The picture most often used to explain the theory describes how a butterfly in a South American rainforest flaps its wings, thus setting off a chain of events which results in a hurricane bursting into life on the other side of the world.

When hope flaps its wings, who knows what will happen? Who knows what changes will happen in our lives, what flowers will bloom, what wonders we will see? Who knows what titanic, wonderful storms will be brewing elsewhere?

■ ■ ■ ■

This is what I want to say at the start of our journey: life can change; things can get better.

To all those who feel as though they are drowning, I say, 'Listen to the beating of the butterfly's wings. It is only a fragile creature, but it has the strength to pull you ashore.'

Hope is the first step along the road to a better life. The truth is that our scenery can change, but only if we start walking.

Of all the rare species that we are so keen on protecting, the one we really must preserve is hope. We must save it from poachers, put it in a reserve, protect it from predators, give it a habitat where it can spread its wings and learn to fly.

BLUE HOPE

- ● Believes that things can change...
- ● Rejects cynicism and never despairs...
- ● Imagines what could be...
- ● And starts to walk.

By the time he had put his clothes on and rushed downstairs, the man was out of breath. He grabbed his bag and a few other essentials, raced out of the back door and across the lawn to the basket – which, he noticed, had completely demolished his roses.

Above him, the balloon filled the sky. Now that he was closer to it, he noticed that its blueness was not of one shade or pattern, but seemed to have all tones within it. One moment it was as light as the sky in spring, the next dark as the dead of night. Looked at one way it was turquoise, but from another angle the fabric rippled sea-blue and mysterious.

'Who ... what...?' he wheezed.

'Hello.' The figure standing in the balloon was small. He had not realized from the bedroom just how tiny the pilot was – why, she could only be four and a half feet high! And so young – a mere child, wearing an outsize leather flying jacket and a woolly blue hat that strongly resembled a tea cosy. Her hands, which were busy pulling at ropes and valves, were clad in what looked like an enormous pair of gardening gloves. She was holding firmly on to one string, which operated a valve on the burner, filling the billowing blue fabric with hot air.

The girl smiled shyly. 'Hello,' she said again. 'Your balloon trip awaits you.'

'You're ... you're just a little girl...' stuttered the man.

'So it would appear,' agreed the girl, laughing.

'No, I meant you're very young.'

'Thank you, I do try.'

'It wasn't a compliment, it was an observation. I meant, well, you're just a child.'

'So it would appear,' she said again.

'Why do you keep saying that?'

The girl did not answer him. Instead, she pulled the cord and sent another burst of hot air into the blue dome.

'Come on,' she said, 'we're wasting time.'

He looked up uncertainly. Something about the way the balloon kept changing colour disturbed him. And now that he came to look at it critically, the balloon was less impressive and a lot more ... well, tatty, than he had thought at first. He could see patches in the canvas where it seemed to have been repaired. The fabric was very old.

'Is it safe?' he asked.

'Nothing in life is safe,' replied the girl. 'Not if you take it seriously.' She laughed as she saw his face. 'But it won't crash, if that's what you mean.'

'I don't know...' He looked again at the balloon, which by this time was the deep blue of space. 'It's a bit old, isn't it?'

The girl laughed. 'Oh, it's ancient!' she cried. 'I must have done thousands of trips in this. I've taken everyone into the blue. Everyone who wanted to go...'

'But look, it's covered in patches.'

'Those,' said the girl in a reproachful voice, 'are professional repairs. I did all the gluing myself.'

'It's not that I'm not willing to trust you...'

Suddenly the girl looked at him. Her eyes seemed as deep as darkness.

'No,' she said. 'You might be right. It might be that you've simply forgotten how to trust. Your supply of trust has dwindled so that you only trust yourself – which is the same as saying you don't trust anyone.'

'I'm just being careful, that's all.'

She thought for a moment. 'Have you ever seen a young bird leave its nest for the first time?' she asked. He shook his head. 'I have,' she continued. 'I've seen baby eagles fly from high mountain ledges; I've watched sparrows leave their trees; and puffins launch themselves from sea cliffs. All of them have the same choice: do I jump or do I stay? You can stay on the ground or you can fly, but you can't do it "carefully". Together we can fly, but you have to climb in yourself. I can't help you.'

He stood there. For a moment his life seemed poised, balanced like the balloon that fluttered and pulled above him. One choice, one word, and the air would escape, the balloon would collapse, and he would be left with mere dreams.

He climbed in.

faith

Each week millions of people gather together to worship. The service usually consists of songs, a talk, some stories from other believers. Then they start to build to the climax – the part of the service where the priest will tell them whether or not their prayers are going to be granted. 'Will today be the day?' they ask. 'Will the hand of God descend and grant me entry to paradise?'

It is a strong faith, for each week only a handful of disciples are chosen. Millions go away unrewarded, unchosen, at least this time. Yet still they believe. Still they make their offerings each week. After all, some-one has to win the Lottery.

To stop believing in God is not the same as to stop believing in gods. It is just that the gods get smaller. The faith remains, but it is redirected, addressed to other deities.

Week by week, millions of people worship the god of money, or the goddess of chance, hoping that their worship will be acceptable, that they will win the jack-pot and be granted the right to enter paradise.

■ ■ ■ ■

I used to believe that I lived in a society that had lost its faith. Now I understand that I live in a society that has lost its faith in God. The distinction is an important one, because every day people put their faith in all manner of gods of their own creation.

People have always created gods. In more primitive times those gods were brutal, elemental. They were gods of carnage and punishment, reflections of the society around them. Recent ages have worshipped different gods, often subtly reshaping their god to fit in with their current view of the world. Some worship money, some power, others worship sex, youth, health, their family ... the list is as long as people's desires.

■ ■ ■ ■

HOW TO CREATE YOUR OWN GOD
● Select an object, an emotion or an activity.
● Put it on a pedestal.
● Expect miracles from it.

■ ■ ■ ■

Humans worship all kinds of gods. The root of the word 'faith' lies in the Latin word *fidere* – to trust. It is all a question of who we trust to make our dreams come true.

Some trust in money, some in sex, some in power. Some worship only their own strength and selfishness. Some worship beauty, some youth, others fashion. The choice is endless. All you need is a pedestal and enough belief to expect your god to answer your prayers.

Each god offers its own special brand of heaven. For money-worshippers, happiness is a million pounds in the bank; for those who worship at the shrine of perpetual youth, it is an anti-ageing cream that works, or a cure for baldness.

It might strike you as a pathetic dream, a pitiful paradise, but that is what we have. The tragedy of people today is the paucity of their dreams. They have little gods, promising little rewards.

■ ■ ■ ■

Some would argue that the loss of faith in the Christian idea of God has been a step forward for humanity, a bold stride into a brave new world.

One look at the world exposes the falseness of that argument. The gilt-age gods have failed us. The gods of political ideologies – the great gods of communism, capitalism and fascism – have been responsible for millions of deaths. In the last 100 years more people have been exterminated, tortured, massacred and brutally killed than in the rest of time put together. Aided by advances in technology (where other 'brutal and uncivilized' ages had swords and axes, we have the cattle prod, the rubber truncheon, the electric chair, the atomic bomb) and motivated by an unswerving faith in the rightness of our cause, we have followed our gods on a wild war dance.

In our personal lives, the worship of money and ambition has led our societies to ever greater extremes. These gods make harsh demands on their followers. Today British workers work the longest hours in Europe. We spend huge amounts of our time at the temples of our gods, and yet we get no reward.

■ ■ ■ ■

There are green-age gods as well. The 'worship' of Gaia, the earth goddess, is as much a matter of faith as the worship of money, sex or power. It is a faith that brings its own set of commandments (recycle, renew, reuse) and which offers its disciples fulfilment through sacrifice.

As with all good religions, there are different levels of adherents. There are the casual churchgoers, like myself, limited to occasional trips to the recycling bins; there are the regular churchgoers, eating only organic food and travelling everywhere by bike; and there are the monks and gurus, vegans tunnelling under road-building schemes or living in yurts somewhere on a Welsh hillside.

The question that has to be asked, though, is whether their worship will bring happiness. It is a noble worship, true, and it can embrace strong and vibrant truths – justice, peace, community, to name a few – but will their god repay them in the end? Will their prayers be answered?

■ ■ ■ ■

I watched a car programme on the TV tonight. They were testing cars fitted with satellite navigation systems, systems devised to plot your route perfectly. Type in the street you are heading for and the navigation system will work out the rest. As you drive along it will talk to you, tell you when to turn left or right, warn you of approaching road works and jams.

The presenter typed in the address and set off. After half an hour she was still in the city, having been taken four miles in the opposite direction. Teething problems, apparently.

Blind faith is like that. Worship without thought or understanding is likely to leave us driving in circles and heading in the wrong direction.

■ ■ ■ ■

We all have gods, and we are all worshippers. Fundamentally, we all want the same thing: rescue. What we want is to be saved. What we want is for something to pull our life out of meaninglessness and monotony and give it purpose. We want a bit of heaven on earth. We want to be rescued from the things that we hate in our world – the loneliness, the

pain, the sadness, the hurt, the anger, the bitterness...
We want to be saved from ourselves.

Too often, however, our gods prove false, and,
instead of being rescued, we are enslaved. The world
is full of people who have found 'salvation' in a guru
or a cult, only to find that instead of being rescued
they have been trapped.

All gods must be questioned. Blind faith is not faith.
It is merely blind.

■ ■ ■ ■

THREE QUESTIONS TO ASK YOUR GOD
● Do you care about me?
● Will you give my life meaning?
● Will you rescue me?

■ ■ ■ ■

It is precisely because their gods have failed them that
people are looking for other answers. The gods of
money and possessions and the gods of recycling and
renewing have not provided all the answers. There is –
there has to be – more.

That is why people are walking. That is why they
are on pilgrimage, why they are looking into the blue.
They know that this earth does not contain the
answers. It promises much, but fails to deliver.

People do not go searching because they are contented, but because they have lost something. The gilt

gods and the green gods have failed us. They promised to give us our dreams, but they failed to deliver. Sometimes all they delivered were nightmares.

Faith should make sense of the world. It should clarify and explain. It should help us to understand ourselves, and give us direction for life. Where false gods are concerned, however, faith leads only to confusion.

There are signs of this confusion everywhere I look. We are a confused society. We are fatter than we have ever been before, yet we are obsessed by dieting. We bemoan the lack of family values in society, yet we work late every night at the office. We shop to cheer ourselves up, and then get depressed at the size of our credit card bills. We yearn for peace and quiet, yet fill our lives with noise and activity.

People are searching. Rejecting the gilt gods and going beyond the green values, they are looking into the blue. From the depths of their confusion, they are looking for a straight path that will lead them home.

■ ■ ■ ■

In the book of Psalms in the Bible, the poet writes that those who make gods will be like them. This is what makes it so important. It is not as if we can worship these gods with impunity. They will change us, for good or evil. Those who worship power become petty tyrants; those who worship money become as hard and unfeeling as a gold coin; those who worship sex end up superficial and shallow, unable to relate to anything except the transient gratification of their desires. Faith inevitably fashions the follower. Society shapes itself after the gods it worships.

The choice of which god to worship might also be expressed as the choice of what we want to be like. If we have a superficial society, it is because we worship superficial gods. If we lack compassion, it is because the gods we worship are hard and uncaring. If we live in a confused and confusing world, it is simply because we have been following the wrong gods.

We can, of course, be a loving, caring society which fights for the underdog and lives in freedom – but we would have to find a god like that to worship.

It is therefore important that we think about the gods we worship. It is the single most important decision of our lives, because one day we will be like them.

■■■■

The junk shop smelled badly of damp. A bedraggled white cat sat on an old sofa. A pile of old magazines teetered precariously in the corner. A tin bath hung from a peg on the wall. Everywhere there was junk – old chairs and tables, boxes of kitchen equipment, vases, tins, old clothes, every item a broken memory.

The jeweller did not expect to find anything of value, but he had time to kill and these places always exerted a kind of fascination for him. Maybe there would be some old costume jewellery, but certainly nothing much. After all, this was a place where all the junk ended up, all the rejected history from people's lives.

'Do you have any jewellery?' he asked.

The old shopkeeper cupped a hand behind his ear. 'You'll have to speak up, sir,' he wheezed. 'I'm a bit hard of hearing.'

'I SAID, DO YOU HAVE ANY JEWELLERY?'

'Jewellery, eh?' The shopkeeper smiled a toothless grin and muttered a few words. 'Yes,' he said, as if he was considering something very carefully. 'I think I've got something, somewhere.'

With that he disappeared into a small room at the back of the shop. The jeweller could hear the sound of boxes being moved. For a moment he considered leaving. After all, this was a waste of time. What was the point of expecting anything of value here? Before he could slip away, the old boy returned with a small leather bag.

'This might interest you, sir,' he whispered. From under the counter he pulled out a black velvet cloth and laid it on the dusty surface. Then he undid the strings on the leather bag and tipped out the contents.

The jeweller stared. The pearl was huge. It was as round as a marble. In the dim light it shone slightly, lustrous and creamy white. It was genuine, too. He knew. He did not have to pick it up. He just knew.

'How much do you want for it?'

The old man smiled a toothless grin. For a moment he did not appear to be answering at all. He was just doodling in the dust on the counter. Then the jeweller realized that he was writing something – a number; a sum.

For the second time he was amazed. 'That ... that's a lot of money,' he said. He knew the pearl was worth it, though.

'Ah, well,' said the shopkeeper. 'Just because something has been discarded doesn't mean it isn't valuable.'

The jeweller nodded. It was the find of a lifetime. It was what he had been searching for all these years. It was worth the price.

He reached inside his pocket for his mobile phone and started to dial the number of his bank.

■ ■ ■ ■

It is time to come clean, to admit my true perspective. Here is the God I believe in:

- A loving, caring father.
- A God who has given his children freedom – even the freedom to reject him.
- A God who will bring all to conclusion, whether we like it or not.
- A God who walked on earth as a man, so knows what I go through every day.
- A God who gives my life meaning.

- A God who is greater than death.
- A God who is my destination.

Today, such a belief is unfashionable, but only because it is specific. Many people believe in a god of sorts, but they cannot bring themselves to believe in one who cares about them, who is willing to be involved in their lives. Instead they talk about a higher power, a life force, an energy...

It is not easy to serve a personal God. It is impossible to serve an impersonal one. For a start, how do you know what it wants? I have no idea what the life force wants me to do next. Perhaps it just wants me to do what I want to do, in which case the life force is just another name for selfishness. I do not want to serve a god that is as petty, selfish and stupid as I am, thank you very much. I already have someone like that in my life, and one is quite enough.

If you think about it, it is really only a belief in a personal God which makes sense of the demands of the green values. Green values insist that I am accountable for the state of the world. But *to whom* am I accountable? Without a personal God, to whom do I answer? The Bible says that we have been put in charge of the earth – not to exploit it, but to steward it, to look after it. We are responsible for this planet, and we will be called to account for our actions. Without someone to call me to account, however, why should I feel responsible for the planet? Without someone who has given me responsibility for looking after his creation, I have no one to answer to and, in reality, I can do what I like.

■ ■ ■ ■

I wanted to keep God back, to reserve him, as it were, for later in this book. I wanted to build up a convincing web of arguments so that at the end I could whip the curtain away to reveal God, waiting there for his cue. I wanted to produce him with a flourish, like a rabbit from a hat; to open the bag and tip the pearl out onto the table. The problem is that, even if I were able to write a book like that, it would be untrue to the nature of God. You cannot keep God as a conclusion, because he is beginning, middle and end. Before I started to write these words, he was there – provoking, inspiring, rebuking, challenging me to find something new about him. Cleave the wood and he is there; tap at the computer keyboard and he keeps popping up.

No, the only thing is to face him right away. To face God is to face the fundamental choice awaiting all human beings. Whom will we follow? In what god will we have faith?

I do not have the space in this little book to rehearse the arguments for the Christian God. All I can do is to start you off, try to get you to think. We all have faith in something. If that is to mean anything, then it has to be faith in something greater than ourselves – something or somebody that will rescue us from the debris of our lives and bring us home; someone we can follow and would love to resemble.

Who else is going to do that if not God? Who else is there to care for us if not the being who made us, shaped us, breathed us into life? The new gods have failed us. Perhaps it is time to give the oldest God of them all a try.

It is only by following a loving, kind and compassionate God that we will become more loving, kind and compassionate ourselves. It is only by following a God who is our friend that we will find the strength to befriend those who need us. It is only by following the creator of the world that we will find the commitment and desire to save it.

■ ■ ■ ■

The reason I became a Christian was not because God was in his heaven. It was because he came to earth. Christians believe that God came to earth in the form of Jesus and that, in this form, he lived and breathed and understood everything that it meant to be a human being. This is a deep truth, because only by becoming a human being could God understand what it was like to be me; what it was like to laugh, cry, weep, sweat, bathe, hug; what it felt like to be rejected, to suffer and to die.

The real test of a false god is this: What is that god willing to do? What will it do for you? Will your god stay aloof and remote, always beckoning you on, but never bringing you home? Or will your god come down and walk by your side?

Faith in a distant god is servitude. Faith in a God who walks alongside us is friendship.

■ ■ ■ ■

Faith is entrepreneurship. It means investing your life in order to gain much, much more. It means looking for a God who will answer our prayers and who will give us what we need and long for. When we find such a God, when we find the real end to our search, then we must give everything we have to this God. We risk our life to gain everything.

As I think about this, I am aware just how risky my life has been. I do not mean physically – generally speaking, the nearest I have ever got to any extreme, high-risk activity was to ride my bike through the traffic outside Waterloo Station in London. The decision to become a Christian is not to be taken lightly, however. If it is to mean anything, then it will cost everything. God loves unconditionally and demands that I should learn to do the same. He loved me when I was his enemy and he demands that I should love others in the same way. He demands that I should surrender all that I am to him.

I do not expect people to turn to my God just because I say so. I do want people to examine their own lives, to identify the gods that they worship and to ask if these gods are really worth their devotion.

We all worship gods of different kinds. Are they good gods? Do they make us better people? Do they bring us happiness and fulfilment? Do they really care about us? If the answer is 'yes', then, and only then, they are indeed worthy of our worship.

To go into the blue is, by its nature, risky. To learn to fly is to step out of the nest, to leave behind the life we have known with all its comfortable illusions. Yet it is the only way. We can look into the blue all we want, but it is only when we leap into it that we will learn to fly. Only then will we soar. Only then will we discover that our dull old world has turned into a bright, shining pearl.

■ ■ ■ ■

BLUE FAITH

- Looks at our gods...
- Examines their promises...
- Asks if they care...
- And risks everything on the one who will truly answer our prayers.

'What's the matter?'

The balloon was not lifting. After the difficulty of deciding whether or not to go, he was a bit annoyed to find that the balloon would not lift off. There was a strong whiff of anticlimax about the whole affair.

'I knew this was stupid!' he muttered to himself. 'Whoever heard of a girl piloting a balloon?'

The girl tugged on the rope to open the valves, but nothing happened.

'We're too heavy,' she said at last. She looked at him accusingly. 'What on earth have you got in that bag?'

He looked down at the small holdall that had been waiting, already packed, for weeks.

'Not much,' he replied. 'My wallet and diary, obviously. A mobile phone. Some pens and paper and a camera. Medical kit, some biscuits, a knife and a bottle of water. A palmtop computer to get my e-mail, and a book and a Walkman and a spare set of clothes.'

She began to giggle.

'Well, I'm just trying to be prepared for all eventualities,' he said, feeling hurt.

'You won't need all that, silly.'

'But I have to take it. It goes everywhere with me.'

'The first rule of flying,' she explained, 'is to try to leave the ground behind. We're never going to get going with all that weight.'

'It's hardly a big bag...'

'It's not the objects themselves,' she said, 'but the weight you give to them. Didn't you know that? Possessions are heavier the more important they are.

I've known people drowned by the weight of one penny. They couldn't leave it behind, you see.'

'But what if something happens?'

She threw her arms in the air. 'Of course something will happen!' she said. 'That's the point! But it won't happen if you insist on carrying the cares of the world with you. We can go everywhere, if only you will leave everything.'

'Oh, all right. But if it's not here when I come back, I shall be really annoyed.'

Reluctantly, he lifted the bag and dropped it over the side of the basket. Almost immediately the balloon began to rise. There was no obvious sensation of movement, rather it seemed as though the earth itself was slipping away, as though the balloon and the basket were the fixed points, and the world was falling away from them.

Within a few seconds the balloon was high above the garden and rising into the sky. Amazingly, all was still. It was as if they were not moving at all. There was no sound, no wind, no sense of motion.

'It's so quiet,' said the man. 'Why can't I feel the wind?'

'Because we're moving with the wind, instead of fighting it.'

He looked over the side to see his beloved bag on the ground below. For a moment the balloon stopped its ascent.

'Stop it!' said the girl. 'Your thoughts are too heavy!'

He looked at her in astonishment. 'Don't be stupid,' he said. 'Thoughts can't be heavy!'

'Yes they can. Just try to forget about all that stuff

on the ground. Empty it all out.'

'I don't want to empty my head, thank you.'

'It's only so that better things can fill it,' she said. 'We're not going to leave it empty. That's no use to anyone. Oh, I know people think that by emptying their heads they're making a difference. But an empty head is useless. A bottle can be full of poison or it can be full of medicine,' she said. 'If you pour the poison out and put the medicine in it will make a difference, but if you leave the bottle empty it helps no one at all. The only thing that bottle is good for is being thrown away. Or recycled.' There was a pause. 'Mind you,' she said, 'some of them believe that one as well.'

The man looked down at his garden, at the bag containing all that he had to do, all that he was. The balloon shuddered slightly.

'You've put on weight again!' snapped the girl. 'Just let yourself be quiet. Let yourself be still.'

He took a deep breath. 'OK,' he said. 'Let's go.'

The balloon began to rise again. They drifted over his house, and for the first time he could see down into his neighbourhood. He saw people scampering about, saw cars queuing in the street, shops full of rush and bustle. He saw the office where he worked each day and he found himself wondering what it was that kept him going there. The town was spread out before him like a map. It was the cartography of his existence, the contours of his life.

'You know,' he said, pointing at each site, 'every morning I leave that house and walk to that bus stop.

The bus drives along that road over there and into the town. I get out and walk to that office building. I've done this for 10 years. Every day. That is what I've become.'

He looked again at the shape of his life and for a moment he almost saw the imprint of footsteps on the paving, as if all those roads were worn down by the people plodding along them.

'What can you see?' asked the girl.

'I see the tracks of people who are caught in the same routine,' he answered. 'I see the way they have worn a rut into the ground doing the same things for so many years.'

'Yes.' She giggled. 'Of course, you don't wear down the pavement if you learn how to skip.'

'It all seems so small from up here,' he said. 'But when I'm down there, everything is so important.'

'That's why you must rise into the blue,' explained the girl. 'Only when you can look down on your life will you see the shape you've made of it. It's all a matter of progression, really. If you want to move on, then first you have to stop.'

'Are you going to keep doing that?' he asked.

'What?'

'Turning the truth upside down.'

She smiled at him. 'Have you ever stood on your head?' she asked. There was a pause. 'No,' she continued, 'stupid question, of course you haven't. Well, when I want people to look at me, I stand on my head. I don't think I'm turning the truth upside down, but if I am it's only to make you look at it more closely.'

The balloon went up.

stillness

The air was full of spring. The sunlight was pale and warm on the rocks, and the blossom on the almond trees threw dappled shadows on the ground.

Impatiently, the farmer had waited for life. The seed had been sown in the grey days, when the frost had still not fled. 'Always a risky undertaking, sowing early,' he thought as he trudged along the path towards the field. Yet he could not wait. He was impatient for life. He loved to see things grow. Every year, at the earliest opportunity, he was out there, casting his seed onto the field.

At the end of the almond grove was a gate, and beyond that was the field itself. He stopped at the gate and looked.

Suddenly aware of his presence, a group of crows rose hurriedly, their wings slapping the air. Always, he thought, there were predators. Always there were birds to take his precious seed away.

As he expected, new life was everywhere. Shoots pushed up through the soil, excited, hopeful. Some seeds lay withered and rootless on the rocks; others grew stunted and useless, choked by the thorns and weeds. There was good soil too, though, and good plants. The soil had taken the seed deep into its heart – long nights of silent movement, the shoots pushing forth, slowly, relentlessly, in the womb of the cold earth.

Sometimes he would come to this gate in the winter and wonder if anything was happening under the surface. Now all his hopes were as green as the spring. New life was being made.

■ ■ ■ ■

I remember, when I was young, spending holidays in Spain and Italy. Much of our time was spent snorkelling in the Mediterranean. Out there it was a different world, calm and peaceful. I would spend hours floating around, spying on this other world. It was a blue world, serene and calm; a world without noise or speed; a world where lush greenery hid creatures of spectacular colours.

Sometimes now I wish that I could get away from life that easily. I wish there was another world to which I could escape, a world where I could be quiet, enjoying the beauty of creation, just floating while the pressures of my daily life drift away.

■ ■ ■ ■

The rise in the popularity of pilgrimage has been mirrored by the rise in the popularity of retreats.

Retreat centres are experiencing a boom as more and more people take time out from their hectic lives.

It is not hard to see why people want 'time out'. The 1990s were the decade when everything started to move with bewildering rapidity. E-mail, faxes and mobile phones led to instant communication with the other side of the globe; shops and supermarkets started 24-hour opening; businesses had to ensure same or next-day delivery; everything had to happen *now*.

Businesses became leaner and 'more efficient' – a euphemism meaning that fewer and fewer staff were asked to do more and more work. The working day increased in length. I have worked in several organizations where there was almost a culture of overwork. I was expected to work long hours at a frantic pace; it was assumed that my diary would be crammed with appointments.

Like a lot of people, I simply became more and more worn out. It is not just at work that the pace appears relentless, either. During the past decade the demands of home life have become ever more strident, especially for working parents who have to hold down a job and look after the kids. Everywhere I look, I see weariness – stressed-out people, rushing around from diary date to diary date, struggling to cope with the conflicting demands of work and family and feeling as if they are failing at both.

Our lives are filled with incessant noise and activity, leaving us all echoing the common phrase, 'There's never enough time to think.' It is this time that we need to recapture – time to think, time to listen, time just to 'be'.

Stillness is a blue value. Like the cool, clear, calm of the sea, it offers us a way out of the rush and bustle of our lives, and a time to experience the restorative powers of true peace.

■ ■ ■ ■

It is not only the pace of life that causes problems, but also the amount of change with which we are expected to cope. It is true to say that in the last century the world changed more dramatically, and more quickly, than in any previous century. The difference between society in 1900 and society in 2000 is immense – far greater than the difference between, say, 1900 and 1800. Indeed, in the last 10 years of the twentieth century, the pace was probably quicker than ever, as computerization and the internet meant dramatic changes in working practices and staffing levels.

Change is inherently stressful. Humans are creatures who cling to tradition, who feel comfortable with routines and patterns in their lives. You can see this at work in children: from a very young age they respond best to structure and pattern, to familiar surroundings and familiar ways of doing things.

Increasingly, however, our lives are characterized by constant upheaval. As the old saying goes,

'Change is here to stay.' People change jobs, homes, relationships, with a frightening rapidity.

Of course, not all change is bad, but all change is, to some extent, disorientating. Every change, no matter how large or small, takes readjustment and, if our lives are permanently changing, then we are always shifting ground, always readjusting. Nothing is ever fixed. We are in danger of becoming psychological nomads, wandering from one point to the next, our minds never settling down.

Rootless, unsettled minds lead to a rootless, unsettled society. Without established relationships, without traditions to bind us, without social structures to offer home and support, without stillness, we become physically and mentally exhausted, unable to focus on truth, unable to do anything very much, except lurch from one crisis to the next.

■ ■ ■ ■

Not all change is bad – but not all change is worthwhile, either. Many of us have experienced the dreaded 'office reorganization', when management consultants suddenly appear brandishing new organizational charts and plans to shift all the desks around. How often has it actually *improved* things? How often has it fundamentally changed the way we work, for the better? Things have not improved. Instead we are left with the same old problems and fears, just expressed in different ways.

What has happened is that life has altered, but not for the better. Things have changed, but they have not been transformed. Change that does not transform us, that does not make our lives better, is mere relocation.

In the film *Total Recall*, Arnold Schwarzenegger goes to visit a travel agent. 'What's the one thing that's always a problem with your holidays?' asks the agent. 'It's you. Wherever you go and however you change your surroundings, you always take you with you. You are always the same.'

So it is with change. I do not want simply to move to another place where I can experience the same problems as before, in better surroundings. I want to be made different. I want my life to be made better. I want to be transformed.

Change is to be welcomed if it is transforming. The caterpillar should embrace change, but only if it results in it becoming a butterfly.

■ ■ ■ ■

Transformation needs more than superficial changes. To be transformed is a deeper process than merely shifting the furniture around or putting up new wallpaper.

The other day on the train I passed a line of perfect, eighteenth-century-style townhouses. Beautiful and elegant, they curved in a sweeping crescent that would have graced old English towns such as Bath or

Cheltenham. But those houses are fakes. They were built last year, not several centuries ago. They were constructed not merely to sell us a house, but to sell us a vision – a dream that we could return to an era of grace, elegance and style.

So often, our response to the pace of life is to tinker with the superficial items. I wonder if the people living in those new-old houses are serene, elegant and graceful? Or are they working every hour they can to meet the mortgage payments?

The more things change, the more we crave for tradition. The faster we head into the future, the more we retreat into the past.

There is nothing wrong with this, except that it is looking in the wrong place. We think that returning to a time when life moved at a more even pace is merely a matter of changing our housing or installing a 'traditional' solid-fuel stove. Our grandparents were delighted to get rid of their range cookers; we covet replicas of such 'homely' appliances and yearn for a traditional cottage garden.

The past, it is true, has many things to teach us about the pace of life, but I doubt we learn much from architecture and range cookers. I think we learn more from attitudes and experiences.

What those in the past did have was time to think. True, only a minority probably exercised the right, but there was surely less bombarding noise. There was time to spend in quiet, there was less movement, more contemplation.

All these things are important. We should learn from the past, rather than try to imitate it.

■ ■ ■ ■

Old steam engines used to have regulators: if the machine built up too much pressure, the regulator valves would open up to let the steam out of the boiler and slow the engine down. Without these regulators, the speed would build and build, and the pressure would grow and grow, until eventually the boiler would explode.

For many people there are no regulators in their lives. There is nothing to let the pressure out. If they keep increasing the pace, then eventually they will explode.

■ ■ ■ ■

Perpetual movement is not just physically wearing, it is psychologically disorientating. It stops us from seeing things clearly, from seeing the truth.

After all, you cannot see a thing truly if you are moving around in a blur. As long as we keep filling our lives with movement, bustle and noise, we will never have to face up to the fact that our lives are actually nothing but movement, bustle and noise. If we keep moving, we will not have to face the truth. We cannot look in the mirror if we will not stand still.

The truth must be faced, however, for no one can

keep moving for ever. Sooner or later we will break down, and the truth in the heart of our life will be even more painful to face. The battle-scarred, punch-drunk face in front of me is *my* face. I was just moving so fast that I never noticed it before.

Just to rest, just to stop for a moment can be a healing experience. At the very least, it can set us on the road to wholeness.

We speak of 'gathering our thoughts together'. In the same way we need to gather the bits of our lives together, to bring them into one piece. Many people live lives of stress and strain, lives which, far from being whole, are broken into many parts: home, office, friends, play... Their lives are shattered by the pace and conflicting demands. We need to stop, to gather the fragments and glue them all together.

A fractured leg cannot heal if the injured person keeps walking around on it. Neither can a fractured life be made whole if you keep running.

We need stillness. It should be a part of our daily diet as much as fibre, carbohydrates and all those vitamins that are listed so carefully on the side of cereal boxes.

This is not easy to achieve. Deliberately taking time out from busy lives is hard to bring about, for it means altering our way of thinking. Indeed, it means putting a high priority on thinking itself. Good things are not necessarily easy, however. It is not easy to have injections, for example, but they might save your life.

What we need is something that was an integral part of the 'old' lifestyle, something which was held sacred by the inhabitants of both elegant townhouses and country cottages. What we need is a Sabbath.

The word 'Sabbath' has rather unfriendly connotations these days. We see it as something restrictive, as a day when fierce, black-clad preachers will bore us all with tales of judgement and damnation. Yet God instituted the Sabbath because he knew that everyone needed to rest. Even God rested. At its core, the principle of the Sabbath is that every six days, humans should simply rest, relax and think.

The Sabbath was meant to be more than just time off. For some people the idea of 'rest' is not helpful, because all that happens is that they sink into a kind of oblivion. Work stops, it is true, but there is nothing positive to put in its place, nothing that enriches and sustains. True rest is about peace, however, and peace is about more than the absence of noise: it is about the presence of health, wholeness, contentment. It is about the presence of God.

Everyone – whether a believer or not – needs a Sabbath, a time of creative stillness, a time of redirection, when we can nourish our souls, renew ourselves and rise again, refreshed.

■ ■ ■ ■

If you would shine as a light, you must recharge your batteries.

■ ■ ■ ■

Stillness gives us time to think, to look at the pattern our lives have assumed. So many people are aware that their life is not what they intended, but as long as they are caught in the bustle and activity they cannot actually remember what it was they wanted in the first place.

It is important to rise above our lives, to examine our goals and dream our dreams. Stillness allows me to refocus on what is important. It allows me to look at the shape my life is assuming and to ask if I really want it to be that way.

It is not just our own lives that we will be considering, however, but also the lives of others around us. We should look at our goals in the light of our relationships. To concentrate merely on what I want is a selfish kind of stillness and one that, in the end, will not lead to any kind of fulfilment.

I had a friend once who used to put aside two hours a week for what he called 'life planning'. This was time to concentrate on what he wanted, where he wanted to go. Now, 15 years later, he is divorced from his wife and separated from his family. It is one thing to concentrate on our dreams, but quite another thing to concentrate on what underpins those dreams. Stillness can lead to self-absorption. What we should pursue is the kind of stillness that brings refreshment to all areas of our lives and all the people that we meet.

■ ■ ■ ■

Stillness is also about listening. I used to teach people 'active listening'. Active listening is when you work hard and really listen to what the other person is saying. Most of the time we do not really listen to other people. We use the time when they are talking to prepare what *we* are going to say next.

In the same way, we can use these times of quietness for active listening. Sometimes we will listen to ourselves, hearing what our hearts want to tell us, listening to the truths that maybe we have let go.

For myself, at any rate, times of stillness are also times of listening to God. He speaks to me through many things: the world around me, a book, a painting, an object, a poem – but it nearly always happens in stillness, at times when I can consider what that object means and what God is trying to say to me through it, at times when I can actively listen to God.

Many Christians say that God often speaks through their reading and thinking about the Bible. Merely to read the Bible – or any literature – is not enough, however. I have to learn to listen to it. What is this passage saying to me? What truths does the writer have to convey?

I used to think that, as a Christian, I had to read

the Bible to learn facts about God, to become more 'expert' at Christianity. I now know that there are no experts, just people who have been listening for longer than others. I now try to read the Bible, not to become more skilled as a Christian, but to hear from God. It is not revision, but conversation.

■ ■ ■ ■

In the Bible, there is a story which exactly illustrates the point and the aim of stillness. It occurs in the book of Exodus and tells how Moses travels through the desert and encounters God in the form of a burning bush. Moses takes off his shoes, because he knows he is on holy ground.

'What is your name?' Moses asks God.

There is silence, then God replies, 'I am.'

The name of God is not 'I was' or 'I will be' or 'I have been once and certainly intend to be in the future'. His name is 'I am'.

The present is holy. We should learn to appreciate it, to live in the moment, to forget the past and future and concentrate on the now. This, I admit, is very difficult. Most of our lives are dominated by the future or the past. Our heads are full of plans we have not set into motion, or dreams we have not fulfilled. Our hearts are noisy with appointments that must be kept and appointments that must be made. We worry about things we cannot control and are weighed down by things we cannot forget.

We cannot find fulfilment if we are always trying to be somewhere else. We cannot have happiness now if we are always planning ways to achieve it in the future. We cannot achieve stillness if we are always rushing into the future at breakneck speed.

Now – the still moment – is important. Every second is to be valued, for we are constantly living on holy ground.

■ ■ ■ ■

We are not, when it comes to it, very good at being 'human beings'. We are better at being 'human will-be's' or worse, 'human have-beens'. We are scared of what we are, preferring to dwell on what we want to be, or what we have been in the past.

What we are, however, is not defined by our actions, either past or present. When I tell people that I am a writer, that is not what I really am. The real me is what happens when I stop writing, when I stop doing anything, when I sit and stop moving – when I am with God.

To be with God is to pray. Most people pray, especially when they are in trouble and, in truth, they have a profound understanding of prayer, for they understand that it is from the heart.

To ask God questions, to bring before him our problems and anxieties, is to experience his friendship. Prayer is greater than that, however.

Prayer is not a conversation, not a cry from the

heart, not a list of requests, not even an utterance of praise or thanks – although it can contain all of those things. Prayer is, first and foremost, a relationship. To pray is to be in the presence of God, to listen to him, to speak to him, to spend time with him, to live our lives with him. In that sense, prayer is a proper and normal occupation for anyone who believes in God.

To think about God, to ask him questions, to find out what he wants for us, that is good. Just to be still before him – that is even better. I love talking to my daughters. I love answering their questions or dealing with their needs. I love it even more when they just climb onto my lap and sit there. No words are needed, no assurances are sought.

■ ■ ■ ■

Society has forgotten how to pray. Or maybe it no longer sees the need. The core of prayer, however – stillness in the now – is something that everyone needs.

This prayerful stillness can be experienced in many ways. To look down from a high mountain, to walk through fields on a summer's day, to experience the quiet joy of companionship: all this is prayer if it is done in an attitude of thankfulness and joy. Sometimes the heart cries out for help. Sometimes the heart calls for answers. Sometimes the heart just sings. All this is prayer if it is directed to God.

Ultimately, such prayer and stillness just seep into our lives. Quietly, imperceptibly, they become a part of us and we carry them with us wherever we go. When the quietness ends, God is still with us. One day, perhaps, we will have brought the stillness of his presence into our very hearts. Then, no matter how fast we move, no matter how busy life gets, we will always be still people, living in the presence of God, living in the now.

■ ■ ■ ■

It is 1 a.m. on a cold, clear February night. The stars are fantastic tonight – billions of points of light, flung into crazy patterns in the dark blue sky. Everywhere is still. Nothing is moving. There is not even a distant sound of traffic.

I should be happy with this right now. I should embrace the moment – and I do. Yet there are other things on my mind.

My mind is racing with thoughts about this book, with all that I want it to be. I do not know if it is any good. I do not know if it has any life. I am scared of what others will think of it, just as I am frequently scared of what others will think of me.

Then a voice whispers to me, 'Be still.'

Yes. I have had a good day. Many words have been written, many thoughts have been thought. I think – I hope – that God has given me something to pass on today. I cannot live in that future, however. I must live in the here and now, and right now ... right now I want to be still. I want to be quiet.

Now there are just two people in the universe: me and the bloke who made it.

Tomorrow will be a busy day. The children will run and shout. The phone will ring. The words will, perhaps, not come easily. But tonight my heart is still. And tomorrow, maybe the stillness will remain with me. Maybe something of the blueness of the night will have seeped into my bones.

It is possible to carry stillness with us, even though we are moving. It is possible to carry the peace of God to others, even though we might be as hard-pressed as they are. It is possible, if we can bring the stillness into the core of our being; if we can take the seed deep under the surface and let it grow

■ ■ ■ ■

My heart is not proud, O LORD,
my eyes are not haughty;
I do not concern myself with great matters
or things too wonderful for me.
But I have stilled and quietened my soul;
like a weaned child with its mother,
like a weaned child is my soul within me.
O Israel, put your hope in the LORD
both now and for evermore.

King David, Psalm 131

■ ■ ■ ■

BLUE STILLNESS

- Stops moving...
- Enjoys a Sabbath...
- Seeks transformation not change...
- And learns how to 'be'.

They drifted over the town.

'Where are we going?' he asked.

*'That's the wrong question to ask of a balloonist,'
replied the girl. 'Never mind about the where. Into the
blue sky, that's all I know. Remember, you can't steer a
balloon. You can't speed it up or slow it down. Up or
down, those are the only choices.'*

'That's not much of a choice,' complained the man.

'Why do you need more?'

*'Choice is good,' he replied. 'The more choice the
better.'*

*'That depends on the choices and the person
choosing,' replied the girl. 'Some choice is good. Too
much variety, and everything is the same.'*

'More headstands?'

*'I only mean,' she said, 'that if you have infinite
choice, then how do you know which choice is right?
The more choices you have, the harder it gets to distinguish between them. In the end you decide that there's
no real difference, and the only thing that matters is
personal preference.'*

*'You're very old-fashioned for someone so young,'
said the man sternly. 'You clearly don't understand
market forces.'*

*'Perhaps not,' answered the girl, staring dreamily
out into the blue sky. 'But what matters more, the
choice or how to choose?'*

*'I don't understand you. Everyone knows that you
choose what suits you best. That's the way to make a
choice.'*

'And what if you choose wrong?'

'Then you make another choice.'

'I prefer to drift along, I think,' she said.

'That's a bit foolish.'

'Sometimes, being a fool is the wisest thing to do. I'm not interested in how much is available, I'm interested in what's the best thing to do.'

'Exactly. I choose what's best for me. I put myself first.'

'Ah, but the first shall be last ... or didn't you know that?'

'Oh, this is getting silly.'

He reached into a pocket and pulled out a handful of maps. He had shelves full of different maps, atlases and guidebooks, each one claiming to be 'authoritative' or 'the most accurate'. He had studied them every night, plotting where he would go on his balloon trip, and that morning, just before leaving, he had managed to stuff a few of them in his pocket. He was aware that the girl was looking quizzically at him, but he ignored her, selected one of the maps and opened it. It was not easy unfolding it, for it was a big map and they were in a small basket, but eventually he spread the sheet out and started to study it.

'Where are we?' he asked after a while.

'Somewhere,' said the girl, helpfully.

'Thanks for your help. I assume you failed your navigation exam.'

'I never took a navigation exam.'

'Why not?'

'I couldn't find the room.'

'You're making fun of me.'

She giggled. 'Somebody has to. Come on, then, what does the map say?'

He stared at the sheet again. The symbols seemed strange. They danced before his eyes. Maybe the altitude was affecting him. 'I don't know. It looks … different. It wasn't like this when I bought it in the shop.'

The map swirled and shook. It seemed to him almost as if the landscape was shifting. Symbols, lines, roads and rivers were wriggling like snakes. He turned it upside down to see if he could make more sense of it, and all the symbols started to slide down the page. As a wood hit the bottom edge, leaves and twigs started to fall out of the map. He could feel his feet getting damp where a small river was dripping on them. Hurriedly he turned the map back up the other way and everything settled more or less back into place.

'What's happening?' he exclaimed. 'Everything's falling out of it!'

'That's because it's not a true map,' said the girl. 'It looks OK from one angle, but look at it from a different direction and everything starts to fall off.'

'I can't even read the names!' he exclaimed. 'Everything looked so clear down at ground level. You could rely on maps there.'

'And now you're discovering that there are maps and there are maps. Not all maps are the same. Not all do what they claim to do.'

'Do you use a map?'

'No. A guidebook, maybe.' She stared out into the sky, happy and content.

In frustration, the man scrunched the map up and threw it onto the floor. Despite his frustration, however, he was determined not to be defeated and he reached into his pocket for his compass. It was an expensive one, the best in the shop – thick and strong with a shiny brass case and a lid which flicked back at the touch of a button. He opened it and held it steady. To his surprise, the needle hopped and quivered and spun round like a propeller.

'What's wrong with this thing? It's pointing in all directions at once!'

'Maybe you're trying to go in all directions at once,' suggested the girl.

'Very funny.'

'I wasn't joking.' She sighed. 'Look, down there a lot of things look the same, but they aren't really. Maybe there are too many directions on your compass, and too many routes on your map. Most maps are of limited use. They tell you where a thing is, but not what it is. They tell you that a place exists, but not if it's true.'

'You're making no sense. How can a place exist if it's not true? It must be real to exist.'

'I didn't say it wasn't real. I said it wasn't true. Your world has difficulty differentiating between the two. Some people think that because something exists it must be true. But not all destinations are good destinations.

Not all choices are good choices. Just because a place exists doesn't mean you'd want to go there.'

Disgusted, he put the compass back in his pocket. 'All right,' he said, 'how am I to choose?'

The girl smiled at him. 'Wisely,' she said. 'Choose wisely.'

'That's a lot of help.'

'Well, think for yourself for once!' she cried. 'It's not a bad thing to have maps, but we need to ask questions about the map. Who made it? What does it really say? What do all the symbols really mean? Where do you really want to go?'

He looked about him. The sky was a brilliant blue. Up above them, the clouds looked like tiny islands, promises of distant lands.

He pointed upwards. 'Up there,' he said. 'I'd like to go up there.'

truth

In the blue, there are two types of truth: insight and authenticity. Insight is the ability to recognize the truth; authenticity is the ability to live it.

Insight looks beyond the surface, seeking to uncover what is real and what is not, seeking to sort, to categorize, to approve. Authenticity seeks to make our 'surface' selves our true selves, removing the need for pretence and evasion.

Insight pierces the hypocrisy of others. Authenticity punctures the hypocrisy of ourselves.

■ ■ ■ ■

From the Office of the Governor
Trial Transcript P7/773

Time: 04:00 hours

Prisoner brought before the Governor. Some signs of beating around the head. Throughout the inter-rogation the prisoner refused to answer simple questions. The following may serve the court as an example:

PILATE: So, are you the King of the Jews?

JESUS: Is that your own idea? Or have you been talking to others about me?

PILATE: Oh, come on. You know full well that your people handed you over to me. Your chief priests. So tell me. One simple question: what is it you have done?

JESUS: My kingdom isn't of this world. If it were, my followers would have fought to prevent my arrest. My kingdom is from another place.

PILATE: So, you are a king then!

JESUS: It is true to say I am a king. In fact, I came into the world to testify to the truth. Everyone who is on truth's side listens to me.

PILATE: Ah, truth … what is truth?

Interrogation terminated: 04:04 hours

■ ■ ■ ■

When Jesus was hauled before the Roman Governor Pontius Pilate some 2,000 years ago, the ostensible purpose was to find out the truth. It was an investigation, with Pilate as policeman, prosecutor, judge and jury. Pilate, to his credit, got the questions right. He asked the three most important questions there were to ask about Jesus: 'Are you the King?' 'What have you done?' 'What is the truth?'

Whether Pilate was serious is another matter. There is a sense of ironic detachment behind his questions. He was, after all, the sophisticated Roman stuck in a provincial backwater with a load of superstitious natives. As for his question about truth, well, maybe he had already decided that there was no truth to be found, only a range of conflicting and apparently random 'truths', each as valid as the other – that is, not valid at all.

Maybe, however, he was really asking. Maybe he really wanted to know, because he could not decide. From what we know of Pilate, he was a weak and ineffectual ruler, but perhaps at this point he was genuinely trying to be decisive. Perhaps, like so many of us, he found himself wide awake at 4 a.m., trying to work out the answers to all his questions.

The truth is probably a bit of both. He wanted to ask the questions, but he was not prepared to stay for the answer. As soon as he had asked his final question, he turned and went out. He asked about truth, but would not stay to listen. He washed his hands of the whole business and let others impose their truth on him. He sacrificed his chance to find real truth for the opportunity of a brief bit of popularity.

■ ■ ■ ■

What Pilate had was knowledge; what he needed was wisdom. He knew the facts, but had no idea what they meant. He was not willing to work at understanding, to put in the deeper thought that leads to wisdom.

I am sitting at my computer. With a tap of a button I can access the worldwide web – millions and millions of pages of information on thousands and thousands of different topics. I can slip a CD-ROM into the CD drive and have instant access to encyclopaedias, dictionaries and photo libraries. I can e-mail correspondents on the other side of the world.

In the next room I have a video and a TV which show me places I can never visit, creatures I will never otherwise see, and feed me all kinds of information. A click of the switch brings up news, constantly updated, 24 hours a day. In the shops there are thousands of magazines to choose from, millions of books, more information than I could ever dream of.

Knowledge is not wisdom, however. Amassing facts does not necessarily lead to understanding. What is needed is the ability to look beyond the facts, to look for patterns, to analyse and understand, to strip away the surface and look to the meaning and implications.

I know the facts. I am washed away with facts. I want something solid to put my feet on. I want wisdom. I want understanding. I want insight.

■ ■ ■ ■

We must learn how to choose. Pilate, in the end, elected to wash his hands of the situation. When faced with the need to make a choice, he chose apathy.

In that sense he was one of the most modern people who ever lived. For Pilate, what mattered was that a choice was made, not the choice itself. He dismissed the idea of an absolute truth, a right choice, and let others make his decisions for him.

'Choice' is a core value of the modern gilt world. 'Customer choice' is the rallying cry of the consumer culture – and the more choice the better.

If you want to see how complicated life has become, try visiting a coffee shop. Where there once was a simple choice between coffee, espresso or cappuccino, there are now hundreds of permutations: latte, mocha, chocolate, and loads of different types of tea. Sometimes I stand in front of the counter like a rabbit caught in headlights, shocked motionless, my life draining away while I try to choose what coffee to drink. Sometimes, all I wish is for the sheer range of choices just to go away for a bit.

In my local coffee shop one day, I overheard a conversation between two students. 'I can't wait until I'm 35,' said a girl. 'By that time my destiny will have been decided. For better or for worse, at least the uncertainty will be out of the way.'

How I wanted to warn her! Never mind 35, at the age of 38 I find that choosing right is more important than ever. But we are not concerned today with choosing right, merely with making a choice. Faced with the bewildering range of alternatives, the act of choosing becomes more important than the choice itself.

To choose wisely takes time and effort – perhaps

more effort than we are willing to expend. Instead we take the easy option, the Pilate route. We decide that there are many views of the truth, and once you decide that there are many truths, it follows that some of them, or even all of them, are expendable.

■ ■ ■ ■

With so much information and so many opinions available, we find it increasingly difficult to distinguish between different 'truths'. Indeed, even when we do choose, we often make that choice on spurious grounds. It is not so much what facts are presented, but who presents them and the way they speak. Politicians are judged not on what they say, but on the way they say it. They willingly play the game, employing 'spin-doctors' to present the facts in the most favourable light.

In place of information, we are receiving a series of adverts. We are becoming an increasingly superficial society, unable to do anything except judge by appearances. We have forgotten how to do anything else. Politicians and the media have been polishing the surface for so long that we are dazzled by the reflection.

■ ■ ■ ■

To seek the truth is to search for what really matters and make it important – the most important thing in our lives. This will not be the same as what society thinks matters. Society's values are not the same as ours. The gilt society values the superficial, the trivial, the transient. We need to go beyond that. The blue society values the deep, the substantial, the eternal.

As it is, we pursue the wrong things. We are bombarded, for example, with powerful and erotic images of what the perfect body should be like, and we pursue that with a seriousness and earnestness that is breathtaking. I wonder, if the media dedicated more effort to showing us perfect souls, would we pursue them as intently? Would we spend more time in prayer and less time down at the gym?

■ ■ ■ ■

The pursuit of truth means looking below the surface, looking into the heart of the issues. The difficulty lies in challenging, questioning, refusing just to accept things on face value, but looking beyond them. Think for yourself, because if you do not, someone else will think for you.

So often we purchase our thoughts 'off the shelf', never questioning accepted wisdom, buying thoughtlessly into common views. The papers, the media, the advertisers, are less interested in truth than in opinion. They want to sell you their view of the world. We must challenge this thoroughly.

It might be argued that, as a Christian, I want people to buy into *my* world view. Well, maybe I do, but not uncritically, not without first testing the truth for themselves. The problem is that most people do not do this. They have decided what they think about Christianity on the basis of limited or partial experience. They have not investigated.

In the Bible, in the book of Acts, Paul the Apostle talked to the Jews in Berea. The Bereans, who are one of my favourite groups in the Bible, listened to what he said and then studied the Scriptures to check if it was true. In other words, they did not just accept what he said because it was Paul speaking, because of the force of his personality. Nor did they reject it for the same reasons. They did not throw it out because of preconceived ideas. They looked it all up for themselves.

I always think this was one of the best responses in the Bible. It has a thoroughness to it. They checked everything Paul said, every day. We must always come back to the facts – we must worry away at them until they present us with the truth underneath.

We have a responsibility to check whether things are true. We must check them against our lives, check them against our Scriptures, check them against the values we know and trust. We should never swallow anything without checking.

I have recently been writing a book of seventeenth-century history, a job which has meant many hundreds of hours of research. In particular, it has meant going back to the original documents and sources, to the historical documents that date from the time itself. Whilst wiser and cleverer heads than mine have offered useful interpretations of those documents, it is still the originals that matter most; it is still the originals that speak directly to me. In the same sense, we should look to the original documents when it comes to judging the truth of Christianity – or, indeed, the truth of other religions.

So many people reject Christianity without first reading what it is all about. They dismiss the Bible, but they have never really read it. When I was 18, I read the Bible properly for the first time. Despite being brought up with the Bible and its stories, it was not until I left home that I sat down and read the original documents. I read one of the Gospels – the mini-biographies of Jesus. In the Gospel of Luke, what I found was not the person I thought I knew, but a living, breathing, real-life man. This was not a make-believe figure, not the esoteric hippy I had always assumed Jesus to be, but a real man, full of passion and vigour and life. He argued and prayed and joked and ate and drank and sweated and … well, he did all the things that the rest of us do. This figure – the historical figure – convinced me in a way that years of churchgoing had failed to do. I went back to the originals and found the most original figure in history.

■ ■ ■ ■

In the eighteenth century they designed houses using popular 'pattern books'. Architects would draw up these pattern books and builders would simply steal the details.

We live lives that are pattern-book lives, copied from other sources – from the TV, from the media, or from our own, ill-thought-out desires. These lives have no truth because they have no depth. We have not designed them ourselves. We have stolen them from other people. It is easier, and simpler, to follow the same pattern as everyone else. We live the same lives and fail in the same ways. If we are unhappy, well, at least we are unhappy together. It is just a bug in the software, a fault in the design. Learn to live with it.

Nowadays, few people build their own houses – or, indeed, buildings of any kind. Everything comes prepackaged, flat-packed. Nothing is ever designed, sourced, built and finished by ourselves. Houses are built by another, to another person's idea of how they should be. Many of us live on estates of houses that all look the same.

We construct our lives using the flimsiest materials. A bit of popular psychology here, a touch of astrology there, a belief that somehow it will all work out. The timber is rotten and the brickwork shoddy, but as long as the facade is OK, we do not mind. As long as the front garden is OK, the back can be like a wilderness.

You see, we do not really believe any of it. None of it is *our* truth, the truth we have discovered, because we have never bothered to look. We would not be like the Bereans and check for ourselves. We would just ask everyone else what they think.

The result of this is not that society becomes more tolerant of different truths, but that it becomes increasingly accepting of untruths. We have nothing to pass on to our children because we have discovered nothing for ourselves. We bought our truths wholesale and we do not know why. How can we explain to our children how to live, if we have no absolutes ourselves?

■ ■ ■ ■

In the book of Proverbs in the Bible, it says, 'The fear of the Lord is the beginning of wisdom.' For many years this saying worried me, conjuring up a scary character – not a wise and gentle teacher, but a stern headmaster, a bureaucrat, more interested in punishing the wrong answer than in encouraging people to seek the truth.

Then, many years after the book of Proverbs was written, along comes Jesus, who tells stories and makes people think, and he presents God in a totally different light. When Jesus talks about God, he talks about him as a loving, forgiving father; as a God who does not want to punish but who waits for us with open arms; as a shepherd who is willing to go far out of his way to rescue one lonely, stupid, lost sheep.

I could never quite reconcile these two images until I realized that, to the Jewish mind, the phrase 'fear of the Lord' meant something quite different. It meant respect; it meant honour; it meant, above all, taking God seriously. That, I think, is why 'the fear of the

Lord' is the root of all wisdom. Taking God seriously, thinking seriously about the existence of God, about whether such a God exists and, if so, what he wants us to do, is the beginning of wisdom.

Whatever happens, we must not trivialize the debate. It is a serious thing. Wisdom begins, not with theories of God, but with fear of God. If God exists and if he loves us, then it is the most important discovery we will ever make. Yet so many people scarcely think about it – they do not 'fear' the Lord, but play games, as though the presence of a creator were a mere philosophical speculation. I cannot make you believe in God. I can only present you with the truth as I know it and trust that you will think seriously about it.

■ ■ ■ ■

This, though, does not answer the question: 'How will we know the truth when we find it?'

I do not know how to answer that question fully, and I have to admit that sometimes those who declare most strongly that they 'have the truth' are those who are most wrong.

The nearest I can get to it is to quote Jesus' words: 'If you hold to my teaching, you are really my disciples. Then you will know the truth, and the truth will set you free.' Real truth sets us free. It is a liberation, a wonderful release. Even the most orthodox dogma, if it does not set us free, is mere deceit.

What, in this context, does it mean to be free?

When we think of freedom today we think of what previous centuries would call 'licence', an unbridled, excessive liberty, the abuse of power, the 'freedom' to do what we want, when we want, to whoever we want. That is the kind of freedom the world peddles today. When people shout, 'I want to be free,' often they mean, 'I want to be selfish.'

That is not freedom, but another kind of enslavement. It has not released us, but has instead locked us in a dungeon of self. Real freedom is the truest expression of who you are. In the words of Scottish novelist George MacDonald, 'Freedom is the unclosing of the idea which lies at our root: the freedom of the rose tree is the rose.'

True freedom, therefore, is the freedom not to be selfish, but to be ourselves. The truth should empower us, release us, show us which road to walk and which path to follow. Truth helps us to blossom into who we should really be. When people really understand the truth of the love of God, they bloom like flowers; their whole life is transformed.

■ ■ ■ ■

What if we do decide it is true? What happened to those Bereans in the Bible who checked and saw that it was good? Many of them, we are told, became believers and thus many of them faced their second test of the truth: to live it out with authenticity.

■ ■ ■ ■

I saw a book the other day which promised to give your house the 'authentic Shaker style'. The Shakers were an American religious sect who lived lives of simplicity and celibacy – but I imagine the authors offering the 'authentic Shaker style' did not mean doing what the Shakers did, i.e. taking a vow of celibacy, living in a community and holding all goods in common. I think it was more a matter of filling your house with beautiful Shaker-style furniture.

Such an approach is lacking in insight. You cannot merely appropriate the furniture and designs of the Shakers whilst ignoring what led to such beautiful work in the first place. Perhaps more than any other community, the Shakers really lived out their beliefs.

What they believed was expressed not only in their words and their writings, but also in the furniture they created, the crafts they designed, the lives they led. The message of their lives was lived out with a thoroughness that challenges us all. When selling their produce, for example, they established a reputation for quality and honesty. In every basket of Shaker fruit or vegetables sent to market, the top, middle and bottom layers were equally good. Rotten produce was ruthlessly weeded out. They agreed never to purchase seeds from elsewhere and mix them with their own product. They sought to be flawless.

They brought the same care and attention to their craftsmanship, where even the backs of their furniture were made as if they would be on view. The Shakers believed in making the hidden parts beautiful, because they believed that God could see them, even if no one else could. They believed that the angels saw the backs of the furniture, so even the hidden parts were beautifully made.

Of course, these days 'authentic' Shaker furniture fetches huge sums at auction, and is bought by people who see the beauty, but most likely have no idea why the things were made to be so beautiful.

If we are to learn from others, we must learn the deep principles rather than just copy the appearance. We live in the gilt age, however, where superficial appearance is everything and where we expect to change our life merely by changing our costume. You do not become holy simply by dressing like a monk. You have to live the life, adopt the whole 'package'.

We think that by changing our clothes, our houses, our possessions, we can achieve an authenticity of life that is sadly missing. Yet these things merely serve to add to the surface – and what is needed is not more surface, but more depth. We have become like one of those Hollywood film lots. From the front the street looks full of fine buildings. Go round behind, however, and you find there is no depth. The doors lead nowhere and the entire building is just a facade.

The challenge to us all is to craft lives where there is no difference in quality between the facade, the public face, and the hidden parts, the bits of our life that we turn to the wall. The challenge is to be like a box of Shaker fruit – true at every level.

■ ■ ■ ■

It is not enough just to know the truth: we have to be the truth too. We have to live our lives with integrity and authenticity. The truths we discover must be more than mere intellectual games, more than just philosophical speculation. They must be principles that can be lived.

I have tried the truth of Christianity in my own life. I have forged it in the furnace of the real world, testing what it has to say against my experience of life and trying to embody its principles. I have failed many times to be 'authentic', but equally, when I have succeeded, this has spoken more strongly to people than any amount of arguing or debate.

It is in living the truth that we test the truth.
It is in living the truth that we are set free.
It is in living the truth that we become truth itself.

■ ■ ■ ■

When a witness takes the stand in court, it is usual to swear on the Bible, to promise 'to tell the truth, the whole truth and nothing but the truth'. Certain Christians, however, do not swear on the Bible. This is not because they do not value the Bible, but because the Bible itself has told them, 'Let your "yes" be "yes" and your "no" be "no".' In other words, you should not need to prove that you are telling the truth. People should know that you tell the truth, because you always tell the truth. Your life should be a living sign of a promise kept.

We are so used to the opposite happening. Governments make promises in the hope that people will soon forget what was promised, or that they can postpone indefinitely the delivery of their commitment. Manufacturers make promises that their goods fail to fulfil.

Every day people say things they do not mean, or make commitments they have no intention of honouring. I have lost track of the number of times people have told me that something is 'in the post' when it is obvious that they are talking nonsense. They do not seem to see it as a problem. They assume that I will understand from their statement that they do not have a clue what has happened to my order and they cannot be bothered to look.

When people do not keep their promises, it is not just that the promise is broken – we also start to lose faith in the words themselves. 'Yes' no longer means 'yes' any more. It means 'maybe'. If we do not act as we say we will, it results in the devaluation of language. Absolutes become conditionals. 'For ever' does not mean 'for ever' any more. It means 'for the foreseeable future'. 'I promise' becomes 'I agree to try until the point when it is no longer in my self-interest'.

This is the problem with so much in politics today. Nobody trusts the words any more, because they have seen so often that what is said and what is done are two totally different things.

The only way to restore faith in the language of commitment is to live in a different way. We have to 'walk the talk'; we have to be people whose words are borne out by our lives. The pursuit of authenticity is nothing less than the restoration of language and meaning, to a point where people know that what we say is trustworthy and true.

■ ■ ■ ■

Anyone can live the truth when the going is easy. When things are hard, however, when everyone is against you, when your life is exposed to ridicule and derision, that is when you will find out whether what you believe really is the truth.

When I travel to London on the train I pass the huge, red-brick hulk of Reading prison. From 1895 to 1897 this forbidding building was the home of Prisoner C.3.3 – or, as he was better known, Oscar Wilde.

Wilde had spent his life covering the world with words, witty words, brilliant as jewels, glittering and clever. He had created a facade for his life, a brightly coloured mask, but it was not the wit, nor the cleverness, that brought him to the truth in the end. It was the removal of the mask, the shame and suffering, that led to understanding.

'Now I find hidden somewhere away in my nature something that tells me nothing in the whole world is meaningless, and suffering least of all,' he wrote. 'That something hidden away in my nature, like a treasure in a field, is humility.'

Out of his prison experiences came his truly great work, *De Profundis*, as well as *The Ballad of Reading Gaol*. Would he have preferred never to have gone to jail? Probably. But he could never have written so truly had he still been wearing his mask.

Suffering is the crucible of truth. We can only subject our truth to the acid test if we are prepared to step into the acid.

■ ■ ■ ■

Truth only partially believed cannot be wholly lived. Ultimately, what we are searching for is a truth that will seize us entirely, a truth that answers our questions, calms our doubts and satisfies our souls.

That is not to say that there will never be any doubt or that more questions will not arise. There will always be questions. Doubt, like the poor, will always be with us. After 20 years as a Christian, I still have questions and difficulties, but I feel that the fundamental truth – the reality of God's love for me – is greater than ever. When I first became a Christian I was fascinated with the doctrine and the detail. Now much of that has fallen away. I have become less interested in theology and more interested in integrity, more concerned with the fundamental issues of Christianity than with the rites, rituals and surface features. It is the deeper issues that are important: who I am, where I am going, how I am to live my life.

Surface truth is partial truth, for it is not rooted in our lives. That is why so many people struggle with the green values: at best they are only a partial truth. They do not give answers to the deeper questions, the questions of purpose and meaning. It is only when people probe beyond the surface of the green values, when they find the deeper answers, that the green values will satisfy. On their own they are just part of the real truth. Only when they are incorporated into the bigger picture – only when we begin to see the truth about our role in creation and our responsibilities to others – do the green values become truly liveable.

■ ■ ■ ■

The visionary novelist George MacDonald was once approached by a woman who asked him to explain, in a few words, the meaning of his book *Phantastes*. He replied that he had written the book with the sole object of giving its meaning.

I do not want to have to explain to people what my life is all about. I want them to understand it through meeting me, through encountering me in their daily lives. I want people to be able to 'read me like a book', and that book should say something to them about the truths I have found and the beliefs that shape my life.

■ ■ ■ ■

Millions of words have been poured out about the meaning of life, but so few people have actually dared to *live* it. Few people have dared to let the truth so possess them that they burn with it, illuminating the world with its light.

At that still point of his life, at 4 a.m., alone in the trial room, Jesus was *demonstrating* the truth, demonstrating the fact that he was willing to die for it. The truth of his life was about to be tested to the full.

In the end Pilate gave up. He went outside, to where the mob was waiting, and offered them the choice: Jesus of Nazareth or Barabbas the Thief. The crowd, unable or unwilling at that moment to think through what they were about to do, listened to the spin-doctors who were mingling amongst them, and chose Barabbas.

Perhaps they thought that it did not really matter. Perhaps they thought that one man was as good as another. Yet their belief that one man was as good as another led to the death of the one man who was better than us all.

But the choice put before that crowd – Christ or Barabbas? God or an ordinary man? – is the choice we all face in our lives. Do we choose Christ or the convict? We cannot dodge the issue. No one can dodge the issue – not Pilate, not the crowd, not anyone.

When we think about the truth, when we consider the need to look deeper, we have also to face the need to look at the deepest fact of all: that there walked on earth a man who claimed not just to speak the truth, but to be the truth. Our response is crucial. We can believe him or reject him. He is, in a sense, at our mercy. Except that, if you accept him, if you believe in him, then you will find that you have been at his mercy all along.

■■■■

BLUE TRUTH

- Seeks insight in order to choose wisely…
- Looks beyond the surface and rejects the superficial…
- Goes back to the original to find what is real…
- And lives it authentically.

For some time they had been floating, riding the thermals across the countryside. Now the landscape puzzled him. He saw things that he recognized, but they looked strange. Some of them, particularly familiar offices and workplaces, seemed much smaller. Others, hills and woods that he dimly recognized, seemed bigger. Some landmarks were missing altogether.

'Where's the ring road?' he asked. He was looking at a city below him, a city he knew very well. 'There's no ring road.' He stared again. 'And the shopping centre has gone... Maybe there's been some kind of calamity. Maybe they've pulled it all down. But it was there only a few days ago, I'm sure.'

He rubbed his eyes. It couldn't have been an earthquake – there was no sign of destruction, and anyway, he would have heard about it. But it wasn't there. It was as if it had never existed.

The girl remained silent. She stared ahead with those strange green eyes, her tiny frame swathed in the outsize clothes, her big blue hat pulled down over her ears. She ... she was the biggest puzzle of all. Sometimes when she laughed she was just a little girl. At other times he stared into her eyes and she seemed as old as the sea.

He looked down again. 'I don't believe it,' he said. 'There!' He pointed a quivering finger at the field below him. 'My old school!'

'That's nice,' she said, dreamily.

'No, you don't understand. It shouldn't be there! They pulled it down 10 years ago.' He jabbed a finger at her. 'Now, you listen here, young lady. What's going on? Is this some kind of joke?'

'Oh no,' she said, seriously. 'Not this bit. No, believe me, it's deadly serious.' She looked down at the school. 'It hasn't been rebuilt,' she continued. 'It hasn't yet been destroyed.'

He stared blankly at her.

'Not all journeys go straight ahead,' she said. 'It depends where the wind blows us.'

'You mean we're in the past?' He laughed. 'Oh, this is getting really silly now. I don't mind compasses that don't work or maps that slide about, but balloons that go back in time? No, there's got to be some other explanation. Maybe it's a film set or something.'

He looked again, but he knew it was real. 'But they pulled it down years ago...' he said.

'They might have destroyed it,' she replied, 'but you never have.'

'If you mean I remember it, of course I do – and not with any fondness, I might add. In fact, I wouldn't mind flying low so I could spit on the place.'

'There are better ways to use spittle,' said the girl.

'Such as?'

She shrugged. 'Licking envelopes, curing blindness, that sort of thing.'

He stared. 'You're mad. And anyway, you don't know what my life was like down there. I have no fond memories of it at all.'

'I never mentioned fond memories. Exactly the opposite. The school exists still because you hate it.'

He looked down. The school seemed closer, more defined. He could make out children playing in the playground, tiny shapes whirling around. There was one child huddled in the corner of the playground – alone, scared.

'You're right. I hate that place. I don't care if it's real or not.'

Memories swirled around him like clouds. The air was thick. The balloon juddered and began to descend, dropping down towards the playground itself.

'What's happening?' he said. 'Why are we going down?'

'We're too heavy,' said the girl. 'You're weighing us down again.'

'What do you mean? I've thrown out virtually everything I brought with me.'

'Not everything. You haven't thrown out the really heavy things,' she said. 'The balloon can't carry the weight of your hatred.'

'I don't want to go down there!'

'You've never left. A part of you has always been trapped there.'

'Please ... let me escape! What do I do?'

The balloon's descent stopped. They hovered, a few hundred feet above the grey tarmac of the school playground. All the experiences of those years rushed up from below. Was she right? Was he still there? Had he really never left?

'You must leave the place behind and move on,' she said quietly. 'You have to try to forgive.'

'I … I can't! I mean, I thought I was going on a balloon trip – I never signed up for this kind of thing. I don't feel like it. It's hardly the time…'

'And when would be a good time? There never is a good time for forgiveness and we never do "feel like it". You think it's easy?' She was almost angry now. 'You think, perhaps, that we wake up in the morning one day, look up at the blue sky and think, "Oh, I'll forgive everyone today – I just feel like it." Forgiveness isn't a feeling, it's an action.'

'It's too hard.'

'Hard, yes. Too hard? That's up to you. Surgery isn't easy, but it saves your life.'

He was sweating. Beneath them the roof of the school glimmered grey, the sun glinting off the slates on the roof.

'But why should I? Why should I forgive them? You don't know what it's like, being bullied every day. Being spat at, punched, kicked. And for what? For being who I was. You don't know what it's like.' She was silent, but he got the feeling that she did know what it was like, only too well. 'Why should I forgive them?'

'Because if you don't, you'll never fly.' She pointed up. 'Look at the balloon. If we're to fly, all of it needs to be filled with air. If some parts of the balloon are torn, then we can't get off the ground. It's the same with us. Hope, faith, love, can't fill us totally if there

are parts that are cut open with bitterness and hate.'
She smiled gently. 'How can we fly if we're always
tethered to the ground?'

He listened to her words and he knew, in his heart,
that she was right.

'Let me tell you the truth. Those boys who bullied
you at school, they've forgotten you. They can't recall
what went on. They would be surprised if anyone told
them. It isn't that they're in some kind of denial, it's just
that they genuinely can't remember. They have enough
of their own shame and bitterness to deal with.'

'I ... it's not fair.'

'It's totally fair. Everyone can be forgiven. Everyone
needs to forgive. What could be fairer than that?'

'But I was the innocent party!'

The girl looked at him and smiled. 'And have you
always been the innocent party?' she asked. 'Or are
there times when you too have been guilty? You can
be forgiven too, you know,' she said, and her voice
was as gentle as a kiss. 'But if you want to be forgiven, you must forgive. It's fair. Some would say it's
more than fair. Some would say it's generous.'

The playground was empty now – all except for
one small ghost, standing in the corner, looking up
into the sky.

'Release him,' she said. 'Let him go. You can't keep
a part of you here for ever.'

Suddenly all of his life seemed to swim past him –
all the hurts that he had suffered and that he had
caused other people to suffer; all the wrongs that were

done to him and the wrongs he had done to others. It was as if he was crushed by it all.

'I ... I don't want it any more,' he said at last. 'Take it away. You're right. It's too heavy. What must I do?'

She smiled and for a moment her eyes closed. Then she leant across to him and kissed him on the cheek.

'Wave to him,' she said. 'Let him go. Give him his freedom.'

The man looked down into the playground, into the face of the lonely little boy, a face so hopeful of release.

'Go,' he whispered. 'Go, please. Go in peace.'

Then the ghost burst into laughter and punched his fist in the air with joy. Suddenly they were rising, soaring into the sky. The school dropped away beneath them and as he looked, it seemed to him that he saw the little boy pick up his bag and run out of the school gate.

'Where's he going?' he whispered.

'Home,' said the girl. 'It's the end of term. He's going home.'

mercy

We live in an unmerciful world. Our gilt society has forgotten how to forgive. It knows only how to punish, how to 'make them pay'. Mercy is a key blue value. Only mercy leads to healing. Only mercy can change the direction of people's lives.

■ ■ ■ ■

Our society has forgotten how to admit mistakes. When was the last time you heard a politician say, 'I'm sorry'? Or a footballer admit, 'Yes, I did actually trip that player up'? Or a chief executive agree, 'Yes, I'm overpaid'?

Nowadays we do not admit that we are to blame, for that is a sign of weakness. We know that if we make mistakes we will not be forgiven. As the lawyers are always advising us: never admit liability.

The result is that we have created a race of people who are locked into their own apparent perfection, who can never admit they are wrong. Relationships are severed rather than one side admitting they might be in the wrong. No one ever, apparently, changes their mind. No one ever admits to making a mistake. It is always 'someone else's fault'.

Of course, deep down, we know this is not true. Deep down, we know that everyone makes mistakes, that we say things we do not mean. We cannot admit it, however. We cannot afford to be found out.

This is hardly surprising when you see how those who do fail are treated. In the gilt society only perfection is allowed. Those who fail are pursued with relentless ruthlessness. Our society is prey to constant witch-hunts: those thought guilty by the press are 'named and shamed'; politicians are relentlessly pursued; the dustbins of the stars are searched, just so that we can find some incriminating evidence.

We take a prurient delight in watching others fall. If we cannot feel good about ourselves, it is always comforting to know that there is someone, somewhere, who feels worse. We are envious of success. The moment someone hits the heights, our first instinct is to pull them down.

All the time, however, there is this nagging doubt, this tiny little voice. What if the same searchlights were turned on us? What if our actions were examined in the smallest detail? What if the tabloids took our lives apart piece by piece? What skeletons would they find in our closet?

Everyone thinks that this judgemental attitude is the sign of a strong society, but in fact the reverse is true.

A truly strong society has the confidence to show

mercy. It has the self-knowledge to admit that we all make mistakes. It has the maturity to help people learn from their mistakes, rather than throw them out into the darkness.

■ ■ ■ ■

The Bible tells the story of a woman brought before Jesus. She had been caught in the act of adultery, which in those days meant death.

Her self-righteous pursuers dragged her in front of Jesus, howling around her like a pack of wolves. 'Teacher, this woman was caught in the act of adultery!' they yelled. 'The law says we are to stone her to death. But what do you say?'

At first Jesus did not answer them. He just bent down and started to write on the ground with his finger. They kept on questioning him. 'What should we do? What have you got to say? Come on, answer the question!'

Eventually, Jesus straightened up and said one simple sentence: 'If any of you is without sin, then let him be the first to throw a stone at her.' Then he bent over and started doodling again.

One can imagine the crowd's reaction. As they thought about it, they realized they were trapped. Not one of them could claim to be perfect. To cast a stone would be to tell a lie. So, cheated of their punishment, they left one by one, the older ones first, until only Jesus and the woman were left.

Eventually he looked up at the tear-stained, frightened woman in front of him. 'Where has everyone gone?' he asked her. 'Has no one condemned you?'

'No one,' she replied.

'Then neither do I condemn you,' said Jesus. 'Go now, and sin no more.'

It is a wonderful story, for it demonstrates the key truth of mercy – that it is always responsible. To forgive does not mean to ignore. Jesus did not say to this woman, 'Go now and carry on exactly as you were before.' He did not say, 'Well, we're all as bad as each other, so let's not worry about it, eh?' Instead he made a demand. He said, 'Go now, and sin no more.'

True forgiveness is healing. It repairs broken lives, pulls people out of the gutter, and sets them on the road to wholeness. It is this facet that we have lost so badly from today's world. We think that to show mercy is to give in, to throw our hands up and say that nothing can be changed. Forgiveness is nothing like that. It is a recognition that everyone goes wrong, everyone makes mistakes. Its aim is to help people put the past behind them and start a new life.

In terms of criminal justice, the judicial system in the West is beginning to recognize that we cannot go on as we have been. There is a growing movement towards 'restorative justice', where the criminal and the victim sit down together in a so-called 'sentencing circle', reflecting on what has happened and identifying the most appropriate punishment. The punishment is decided by those really involved, along with the police, the probation service and members of the defendant's family.

Restorative justice restores. Its aim is not to punish, but to heal. This is emphatically not an easy option. For many criminals, the one thing that truly shocks them is meeting the person they have harmed and having to face the personal impact of what they have done. It is a merciful kind of justice, however, because its aim is change rather than punishment. It aims to change, not to punish, the offender.

I am not naive. I accept that there are many crimes where this 'restorative' approach would not be suitable. I know that there are people who should be locked away, for the safety of society. I understand that many criminals will not change. They have gone too far, locked into their own worlds of violence, lies and deceit. But what about those who might be changed? What about those who would respond to mercy if it were offered? Should we throw them in with the others? Should we give up on them? Should we condemn them to overcrowded prisons which are little more than colleges for criminals? We have hundreds of thousands of people who believe that, since society has given up on them, they will give up on society.

Perhaps, with a little wisely applied mercy, there might be a better way than simply filling our prisons to overflowing. I believe in justice. I believe the innocent should be protected and the guilty convicted. I also believe that we cannot go on as we are. Sooner or later, we must have the strength to show mercy.

■ ■ ■ ■

We have forgotten how to forgive because we have forgotten how to be forgiven. We cannot show mercy because we no longer receive mercy. Forgiveness must be learnt, but we have no teachers. Since there is no one to forgive us, no one to wipe the stains from our lives, we belittle and besmirch others.

We are living in a state of denial, for the truth is that all of us need mercy every day. Each day of our lives we commit 'crimes' against others – small crimes, perhaps, but crimes nevertheless. We snap out a swearword, spread false rumours, betray confidences, trash someone else's reputation. Then there are the 'bigger' crimes – fist fights, petty theft, adultery. Nothing, it is true, that will worry the courts, but activities that hurt and damage others.

Jesus' penetrating question still strikes us after 2,000 years: 'Is there anyone here who has the right to cast a stone?' Is there anyone who has not been guilty of lying or pilfering or fighting or abuse?

We may not be housebreakers, but we have broken hearts. We may not have been convicted of fraud, but there are plenty of times when our behaviour has been dishonest. We may not have physically attacked anyone, but we have beaten them up with our words. We may not have stolen money, but we have robbed others of their reputation by slandering their name. This might appear trivial, but thoughts are not trivial things. They are as hard as nails.

Jesus spoke about the power of thoughts. 'You have heard it said, "Do not commit adultery," he said, 'but I tell you that anyone who looks at a woman lustfully has already committed adultery with her in his heart.' To wish someone dead is to kill them in my mind, to commit a kind of psychological murder. To lie about someone is to defraud them. Inside our heads, we are all criminals.

Who will forgive us for our crimes? What court will grant us mercy? What sentencing circle will there be for us? How can we wipe the slate clean and start again? Where are we to learn the art of being merciful?

■ ■ ■ ■

A young man decides that he wants to live his own life. Tired of his life on the farm, he asks his father to buy out his share of the business and goes off to spend the money in the city.

In the city everything looks wonderful, feels wonderful and costs a lot. He makes friends who help him spend his money – and wow, does he spend money! The drinks are more expensive, the food more costly. In fact, everything he wants costs him a great deal more than he had ever imagined. Soon he has run out of cash. His friends – the new friends he thought he could trust – have disappeared. He has to seek a job.

Jobs are hard to come by, however, and soon he is sleeping rough, begging in street doorways, scouring rubbish bins for the food that others have discarded.

Then, one day, a woman takes pity on him. She lifts him from the street, takes him to a café, buys him a meal and a warm drink. Something in her eyes reminds him of someone...

He remembers his father and all that he has left behind at home. He thinks how wonderful it would be to go there now, just to work as part of the farm team. Not to be a son – that is more than he can expect – but at least to be somewhere where he can belong.

He sets off for home. As he walks, he prepares a short speech, ready for his father. His father will be proud, haughty, gracious perhaps, but keen to make a point. 'Father, I have sinned against heaven and against you. I am no longer worthy to be called your son...' He rehearses this speech again and again on the long road back to his home.

Then, as he approaches his home, he sees something in the distance. Something is throwing up dust on the road; something is rushing towards him.

It is his father. His father is running, and as he runs, the people by the side of the road laugh and point, shouting at him to slow down. Dogs run alongside the old man, barking and yapping. And still he runs, for he can see his son coming home.

He runs right up to his son, throws his arms around the boy and weeps with joy. The boy begins his prepared speech, the dramatic nature of which is slightly ruined due to the fact that he is muffled in his father's arms and the old man will not stop snuffling with joy. At the end of his speech, his carefully prepared peace offering, it is as if the old man has not heard him at all. Instead he leads the boy back up the road, and invites all those who were laughing at his antics to come and join them.

'Why are you so pleased, old man?' they say. 'Isn't this the wastrel, the boy who thought he knew it all?'

The old man, still crying, says, 'Knew it all? He knew enough to come home – that's all that matters! He was dead, and now he's alive. Come to the party!'

■ ■ ■ ■

Jesus rarely told people they were bad. Instead he offered them the opportunity to be good. He told people that God loved them and promised them forgiveness. He did make demands – he asked people to change their lives. Instead of making people feel the hopelessness of their guilt, however, he opened their eyes to the possibility of being good. He spoke much more about love than he did about punishment.

He spoke about love because true forgiveness can only come from love. Jesus described a God who wants to run towards us, who is waiting to see us on the road that leads to him. All we have to do to wipe the slate clean is to ask him, to bring to him a speech very like the boy in the story: we have forgotten about you, we have hurt you, just take us back... And he will throw a party for us as well.

Ask and it will be given to you. Knock and the door will be opened. Yes, the door will be thrown open, knocked off its hinges, flung back so quickly and so hard that the wood splinters and the plaster cracks. We think God forgives reluctantly, but in fact he does it, as he does all things, exuberantly, joyously, gloriously. He runs down the road, sandals flying off, robes flapping, because he has seen us coming from a long way off. Before we can even get the words out of our mouths, we are swept up in his love and whisked away to the party. When it comes to forgiveness, God has no decorum at all.

■ ■ ■ ■

To forgive and be forgiven is a blue value. Without forgiveness there can be no growth. How do we learn if not through trial and error? But if every error means that we are cut down, we cannot grow.

Forgiveness does not mean that I accept my sins and failings, but that I can learn from them, leave them behind and move on. Forgiveness is the basis of self-knowledge, for it allows us to acknowledge our failings and to rise above them – not by our own hand, but lifted by the hand of God.

■ ■ ■ ■

In my mind there is a rogues' gallery – a little book of names and faces, people who have wounded or hurt me over the years, people on whom, secretly, I would love to take revenge some day. I am sick of this book.

I do not want to read it any more. In the dark of the night, however, when my guard is down, I flick through the pages...

■ ■ ■ ■

I went to give a talk at a church one day and got talking to a man afterwards over coffee. He told me that he used to work for a well-known Christian organization, but that, according to him, they had sacked him because he had 'come up with a way of saving them money'. Somehow I think this was a re-edited version of events, but even had I wanted to challenge it, I could not, because he was away – ranting on about the injustice of it all, and how it had ruined his life, and how could people behave so badly? Eventually there was a pause.

'When did this happen?' I asked

'About 15 years ago,' he replied.

Now, 15 years is a long time for anyone to be carrying around the bitterness of failure. It was clear that during those years he had carried this horrible event around with him like a strange war wound. He would approach every unsuspecting visitor and shove the wound in their face, shocking his chosen victim with his tale of injustice and ingratitude. In all that time, the scar had remained infected and festering. How could it not, when he insisted on ripping the bandages off at every opportunity?

In the Bible, the injunctions on us to forgive other

people when they harm us are among the most difficult commands to follow. We are the wronged party, the innocent victim. Why should we forgive? We want justice. We want revenge. If we cannot have justice (and in most cases we cannot, because the hurts happened so long ago) we will have attention. Like Coleridge's Ancient Mariner, we fix a passing stranger with a beady eye and prepare to roll out the long list of our injuries.

How difficult it is truly to forgive. We all cling to our grievances, nurse them, feed them in secret. Outwardly, of course, we give the appearance of having 'got over it'. 'It's all in the past,' we say. 'Forgive and forget…' But then, in our dark hours, we bring out the secret from the place where it has been hidden and roll it around in our minds.

'If only I'd said that…'

'If only they knew what the truth was…'

'If only I could tell them, just for one minute, what they've done to me. I'd make them squirm.'

The truth, of course, is that 'they' are not squirming. We are.

■ ■ ■ ■

Forgiveness is perhaps the most difficult, and the most vital, value we have to learn. Without forgiveness, we can never really move on. If we are to go on a journey, then all of us has to move. No traveller can leave a part of themselves behind. The hurts that people inflict on us are many and varied, but the solution is always the same: forgive and you will be forgiven.

We cannot say to God, 'You can have all these sins, but this wound, this bitterness, this hurt I'm keeping for my own use.' You can never be totally forgiven if there is always a part of you holding back. You can never be totally clean if you always leave one leg hanging out of the bath.

Jesus was insistent about the need for forgiveness, because bitterness is so dangerous. It can destroy you in the end. All evil begins as a tiny thing, a thought, a memory. It is a splinter in our mind which, if not plucked out, grows septic until the whole of our body is infected.

We must forgive, because only that will prove that we are serious about starting again. Jesus insists that we change our lives – and that means starting to act like him. His forgiveness was so great that it embraced those who betrayed and killed him. It embraces us all.

You cannot be made clean while you are deliberately nurturing hatred in your heart. You cannot be made whole while you are still keeping the wounds open.

If I want to 'sin no more', I have to start with myself. It is not easy. I make many mistakes each day. I try to be like Jesus and I fail so often. That is not the point, though. The point is that I am walking – all right, stumbling – in the right direction. There will be setbacks. Every healing process has its setbacks. What matters is my determination to keep on going. What matters is that I continually accept God's forgiveness, and continually seek to forgive others.

■ ■ ■ ■

And the end of it all is that I have got to forgive you. I must do so. I don't write this letter to put bitterness into your heart, but to pluck it out of mine. For my own sake I must forgive you.
Oscar Wilde, *De Profundis*

■ ■ ■ ■

I do not have God's nature – or, at least, I do not have enough of his nature. I do not rush to forgive. I am, however, beginning to understand that forgiveness is an act of will, empowered by love.

All of us carry heavy burdens. We are scared of the future and scarred by the past.

■ ■ ■ ■

Let me take you back to my rogues' gallery, my hall of shame.

I do not love these people, but I try to love God.

I do not feel like forgiving, but then I suppose no one ever really feels like forgiving someone else. Just the opposite. We feel like shouting at them, hitting them, humiliating them, gaining revenge. What we have to do, however, is to grit our teeth and tell ourselves that we forgive them.

If I cannot rush towards these faces in my rogues' gallery, then I can at least start to walk down the road. To inch towards forgiveness is at least to move in the right direction.

We must go as far as we can. As we forgive, so we learn to be forgiven. As we love, so we learn to be loved. As we walk, so we learn to run.

What I must also do is avoid dwelling on the hurts. I cannot, try as I might, predict when these thoughts will arise. Time, it is said, is a great healer. I am not sure if that is the case. I think time is more like an interior decorator. Over the years the decorator puts more and more paper over the crack, but beneath all the paint the crack is still there. One tiny tremor, and the paper peels away, the paint falls off, and the crack is on display again, as fresh and obvious as ever.

Those injuries will come back to me, but that does not mean I should dwell on them, or strip the paper away myself. The thoughts will arise – let them go.

Or, better still, pray for them. Today I conjured up those images – some of them as old as my schooldays – and I prayed for each and every one of them. It was good. It was healing.

It is difficult, after all, to hate someone when you are giving them a present.

■ ■ ■ ■

BLUE MERCY

- Acts with wisdom and makes demands…
- Seek restoration rather than punishment…
- Learns how to be forgiven…
- And how to forgive.

The sun shone through the balloon, turning it into a great blue window, a huge lamp of light and colour.

Looking around, the man began to wonder if something was happening to his eyesight. The air stung his eyes like antiseptic.

'It must be the air up here,' he said. 'Everything is so clear, so bright. The colours...'

'The air is good,' agreed the girl. 'It's free from everything that pollutes your vision down on earth.'

'Ah yes, that would be it. All that lead and petrol fumes and smog.'

'I was thinking more of things like cynicism and weariness and overfamiliarity.'

He sighed. 'Maybe it's just me,' he said, 'but I've never noticed the availability of uncynical petrol on the petrol station forecourt. I've never seen all those weariness particles clogging the atmosphere.'

'You haven't?' said the girl, either not noticing or ignoring his sarcasm. 'I see it all the time. The air on earth is full of things that affect the way you see things. Cynicism, bigotry, hatred, bitterness – they take all the colour from the world. Maybe you were just getting old.'

'I'm not that old.'

'You don't have to be. It doesn't take long before your eyesight starts to fail. The little children, they can see the colours and the wonder. Then you get older and nothing shines any more.'

They flew on. Stately. Serene.

'It's certainly a wonderful world,' said the man.

Below him the earth rippled like fabric, patchworked green and brown, deep red and sandy yellow. They passed over valleys with winding rivers, the water running blue and brown and white across sparkling rocks; over forests of pine, oak and ash, ancient and huge, their leaves rustling with the wind of time; over heathland and mountainside, where the sun-warmed earth threw out scents of lilac and wild thyme. They flew over islands and archipelagos, reefs of emerald green, white beaches and cobalt-blue seas.

From the depths of the ocean, a whale's back broke the foamy waters. In a clearing in the forest he saw a deer stand, quivering and alert.

There were other things as well: machinery and buildings, villages of grey stone folded amongst the countryside, mud huts spotted across the brick-red earth, caravans moving over the burnt desert sands, boats on the ocean, bridges spanning vast, muddy estuaries, castles and cottages, temples and tombs, gardens and roads and people, people everywhere.

'Such beauty,' said the girl. 'It gets me every time.' She pulled out a huge and grubby handkerchief and blew her nose. 'The world is a signpost,' she snuffled, 'but we've forgotten how to read the letters.'

After a while, the air turned colder, brittle with frost. Mountains slid by below them, their grey rock and green vegetation giving way to sheets of ice. Then slowly, silently, it began to snow, the flakes fluttering moth-like onto the man's face and hands. He gazed open-mouthed at the silent fury of the snowflakes whirling in their ecstatic cascade. Millions and millions of snowflakes, yet each one different, fragments of complexity, random messages from a magnificently rich universe.

'The world is so big and wonderful and strange,' he said, staring at a snowflake in his hand.

'Have you ever thought,' said the girl, shaking the snow from her hat, 'what the chances are of that snowflake existing?'

'But it does exist.'

'Well, it does now, silly. But before. What are the chances? Almost as small as the chances of you existing.'

'But I do exist. You're not going to tell me that I'm just a dream?'

'No,' said the girl. 'Not yet, at any rate. No, I meant the chances of you being here, right now. Look at you – as unique and improbable as a snowflake.'

'I don't feel unique. I feel like everyone else.'

'But you're not. You're utterly different. I mean, never mind the obvious things – the fingerprints and the DNA and the retina patterns and all that. I mean, inside.'

'You're telling me I have a unique spleen.'

She laughed. 'I'm telling you that you have a unique soul. No one has ever thought like you. No one has ever lived your life or seen things through your eyes. You're one in a billion. One in billions of billions. You're almost totally improbable.'

He laughed. 'I suppose I am.'

As silently as it had come, the snow stopped. Out ahead loomed a huge mountain range, blue-grey in the setting sun. A bird flew by, silent and dark, but with wings that flashed golden and white.

'Glorious...' he said. 'I never really noticed all this before.'

'No,' said the girl simply. 'Most people don't. But each of these creatures is wonderful, just as every human being is wonderful. Just as, in fact, every hair on every head is a miracle of precise engineering. Everything is wonderful,' she said. 'And we should wonder about everything.'

He turned again to look at the mountain, silhouetted in the sinking sun. For the first time he noticed how dark the sky was, and how the clouds were beginning to roll towards them.

wonder

A dictionary definition:

wonder *vb.* 1. to feel or be affected with wonder; to be struck with surprise or astonishment; to marvel.

■ ■ ■ ■

The world has lost its sense of wonder. In an age when the TV camera has explored the depths of the ocean and the height of the sky, familiarity has bred contempt. We have dissected the earth and mounted it for display in a museum.

Wonder is a blue value, and without it we cannot see the world for what it really is. We need to rekindle that sense of awe and excitement which can be engendered by the smallest of things. We need to examine what lies all around us, to get excited about it and to ask what it means.

Jesus said, 'I tell you the truth: anyone who will not receive the kingdom of God like a little child will never enter it.'

Wonder comes naturally to children. Perhaps that is

why Jesus continually exhorted his followers to learn from them. We must learn the right things, of course. God does not call us to be childish, but childlike. We are not to return to the petty squabbles of the play-ground or nursery, but to the sense of excitement and fun and play.

■ ■ ■ ■

On the wall of my study there is a map of the world. It is a copy of the Mappa Mundi, which was drawn about 700 years ago by a monk called Richard of Haldingham. For Richard, the world was a wonderful place. Working in the childhood of the sciences, he found wonderful things to be discovered, revealed and drawn.

To the modern eye, everything about the map is strange. There is no America or Australia. The world is the wrong way up. (Medieval theologians believed that east was the holy direction. Eden was in the far east, the sun rose in the east, so east was obviously the most important direction. East, therefore, was put at the top of the map.) The earth is a flat disc, with Jerusalem – to the medieval mind the most important city in history – right in the middle.

The rest of the world is drawn accordingly, with Britain bottom left and the uncharted mysteries of Africa filling the right-hand side. The map is filled out not only with all the principal cities, but with illustrations show-ing events from the Bible, as well as mythical beasts, stories from old romances, recent historical events and all manner of strange and fabulous human beings. Over it all sits God in splendour, surrounded by angels.

As a map it scores zero for accuracy and basic geographical understanding. I do not think that was what Richard was trying to do, however. Richard's aim was not to produce a chart, but to make a statement. The world was God's world, every inch of it rich in significance and meaning. You cannot walk on the earth without kicking up the dust of wonder.

There are many ways to look at the world. We can measure it with the implements of reason. We can divide it up into nations and borders. We can also look at it through the lens of wonder.

■ ■ ■ ■

To the medieval map-makers, east was the holy direction. Go towards the east, and eventually you reach Jerusalem, the holy city. Continue far enough, and you come to Eden, guarded in the Mappa Mundi by an angel with a fiery sword. And beyond Eden? Beyond Eden, at the top of the map, sits God.

The Latin word for east is *oriens*, from which we get other 'eastern' words such as Orient and oriental. We also get the idea of orientation. To reorientate, literally, is to turn towards the sun.

The search for blue values is a true reorientation. It is to turn away from darkness and look into the dawn sky and the rising sun. It is to face the opposite direction from our empty 'western' values, not to find those of the physical east, but those of the true east, the holy east. If we would truly reorientate our lives, we must turn our faces to God.

■ ■ ■ ■

The enemies of wonder are arrogance, cynicism and overfamiliarity. Blessed are the childlike, for they shall be continually amazed.

It is a sad thing to look into the eyes of someone who has lost their wonder. They are living in twilight. They have grown old too quickly. Our culture kills childhood. Children grow up so quickly – some in cruel and painful ways through broken homes and abuse, others through continual exposure to all the tawdry images that the 'adult' world thinks are so important. Many six-year-old girls are worried about their weight. I have met seven-year-old boys who are cynical and bitter.

Recent evidence has shown that children are entering puberty far earlier than their forebears did. It is as if their bodies are speeding up, accelerating into adulthood before they are properly prepared for it. Similar things are happening with their minds. A continuous diet of 'adult' messages has poisoned their childhood with cynicism, selfishness and doubt.

■ ■ ■ ■

Pain, sadness, loneliness, hunger, poverty – all these kill our sense of wonder. We are not colour blind, but wonder blind. It is there, but we cannot see it. After all, it is difficult to see the sunlight when you are living in the shadow.

■ ■ ■ ■

Part of healing the sick and feeding the poor is not merely to save their lives but to help them live. Our aim – the aim of all aid and development work – should not merely be limited to providing physical and material wellbeing. We should also be aiming to give people, all people, the chance to live and grow, to be loved and to see the world for the beautiful place that it is.

My first responsibility to a starving child is to give her food and medicine. My second is to give her back her childhood.

■ ■ ■ ■

There used to be an advert on TV for Pepsi Max, featuring four young men. When they are offered chances to go bungee-jumping, white-water rafting and other white-knuckle adventures, they react in a bored, 'been there, seen it, done it' kind of way. Eventually, of course, they are presented with the amazing Pepsi Max and are astonished at this new and thrilling experience. I doubt that, as an experience,

Pepsi Max rates higher than bungee-jumping, but it illustrates only too well the desperation with which our society seeks thrills and excitement.

The advert was based on the idea that everyday life is boring and prosaic, unable to offer us the thrills that we deserve and have come to expect. We have generated a culture which rejects the ordinary as being worthless and instead is constantly on the search for the new and the exciting. Only the 'special' has any merit.

To call someone 'modern' these days is to imply that they are old, cynical and jaded. We have become like fat old gourmets, our palates dulled through years of overindulgence. We have forgotten how to taste.

■ ■ ■ ■

I have been watching the sparrows feeding on the tree in front of my study. They are nothing special, one of the commonest bird species in the area, yet their feeding has a kind of grace about it, a kind of neat economy.

I remember bird-watching in Norfolk, looking for the rare honey buzzards. The site was full of serious bird-watchers – huge, expensive telescopes, pagers and mobile phones to alert them to the latest rarity, significantly large anoraks.

There was no sign of the buzzards, but out of the bushes came a yellowhammer, glorious and glittering with gold. 'Look,' I said, 'a yellowhammer!'

I looked round for a response, but all I got was a sad look and a bored shrug. Yellowhammers are common birds. It may be a rarity for honey buzzards to mate in the UK, but apparently yellowhammers are at it all the time.

Yellowhammers are both common and glorious. So are robins. So are sparrows. So are mallards. So are people.

■ ■ ■ ■

Christianity is sometimes accused of being other-worldly. The truth is that it is relentlessly this-worldly. The entire basis of Christianity is that God walked this earth, and we can encounter him here and now, on this precious, flawed world.

The Eastern mystic might say that this world is a veil of illusion. The Christian mystic says that this world is wonderfully, intricately, painfully real. Christianity does not despise the body, the corporeal, the substantial. Matter is good because God invented it. Bodies are not to be despised if Jesus the Son of God thought it good enough to inhabit one.

Jesus ate bread and drank wine. Even after his return from the grave, he thought it a good thing to serve his disciples some fish at a beach barbecue. Flesh, apparently, is good. Especially fish flesh. Grilled.

■ ■ ■ ■

My children have taught me a lot about wonder. A piece of paper can be miraculous, the colour of a flower a huge talking point. Just seeing something pink reduces them to paroxysms of excitement.

When God chose to mark the significant occasions, he did so with ordinary things, everyday items like bread and wine. When God is present, they are signs of wonder.

For God, the ordinary becomes special, the world becomes alive. Nowhere is this more true than with people. The Bible says that people are potentially immortal, that we can all choose to live with God. Thus there are no such things as 'mere human beings'. Everyone is a potential angel.

Rightly understood, there is nothing ordinary about the world, nor about its inhabitants. Each is a unique and precious work of art. Each is, in some way, the signature of the creator.

Miracles are all around us. The miracles or Jesus are not surprising when we consider what miracles God has already set in motion. Turning water into wine happens all the time: that is what God invented grapes for. It is just that sometimes, if he likes, he can do it quickly. This world is soaked in the miraculous. If you want to see a miracle, get up and watch the sunrise.

■ ■ ■ ■

I have been sitting here trying to work out how many ancestors I have, and I have been forced to the conclusion that my existence is little short of miraculous. The maths alone is staggering: I had 4 grandparents, 8 great-grandparents, 16 great-great-grandparents, and so on. Only a few generations back, and I have many thousands of ancestors. Think of the miracle needed to bring all those people together, the miracle that none of them was killed, none of them died, before they could conceive. They survived wars, disease, famine and poverty.

Not only that, but we are also, individually, the product of an enormously unlikely event. Out of millions of sperm, one made it through. Just one. And that one became a human being, a unique human being. Everyone on earth is different. Everyone on earth has his or her own distinctive fingerprints, DNA, retina patterns...

We are all, statistically speaking, extremely unlikely indeed.

■ ■ ■ ■

There are two ways to live your life: one is as though nothing is a miracle; the other is as though everything is a miracle.

Albert Einstein

■ ■ ■ ■

Most people would agree that human lives are precious, that people are special. The real question is, *why* are they special? What is it that makes humans worth bothering about? What is it that makes us care for people on the other side of the earth? What makes us want to do something to help them when we see they are in distress?

Scientifically speaking, human beings are just collections of chemicals, arrangements of sinew and muscle and bone. Looked at with scientific eyes, there is really nothing very special about us at all. We are just another animal – albeit one with a specialized brain and opposable thumbs.

None of us really feels this way, however. There is something indefinably precious about us, something that can only be described in mystical terms. We can create wonderful works of art, we are capable of deep emotion, we can live lives of sacrifice and grace. There is something about us that provokes compassion.

What is it that makes us feel this way? What is it that makes me care about the fate of a child on the other side of the world – care enough to give money, or seek justice, or campaign on her behalf? After all, on one level, she means nothing to me. I do not know her name: she is just a face on a TV screen or in a magazine. That is not the level that makes us truly human. On a deeper level, I feel for her because we are all related.

The green values talk about human beings' relationship with each other, the complex web of relationships in the 'global village'. We tend to talk of this as an economic relationship, but that is to cheapen the true nature of the relationship. We recognize that people should be treated with dignity, respect and fairness, not for political or philosophical reasons, but for emotional reasons. It hurts us to see our family treated without respect or fairness.

We are not just neighbours in the global village, but relatives. It is only when we see each and every person on this planet as a child of God that we can understand why we feel so strongly about people we have never met and will never meet.

We do feel strongly about them. We all feel instinctively that humanity should be treated with respect. We all flinch when the weak and the powerless are abused. We fight for the rights of those who are weaker than us. It is not because we are part of the same species, it is because we are part of the same family. We share not just the same biology, but the same Father.

■ ■ ■ ■

Only when we see people as children of God, filled with wonder and fully wonderful, will we start to treat them with fairness and justice. To recognize God in them is to see what makes humans special. We have a soul. We have a sense of the eternal, a sense of the mystery of life. We are more than mere flesh and blood.

The Bible says that all of us have the potential to

live for ever and that every human being is 'fearfully and wonderfully made'. Everyone is a child of God.

This potential immortality is the only thing which makes human beings special. After all, without it, what is there to mark us out? If no human being is special, then why should we care so much about each other?

It is a crime that an immortal soul should be allowed to grow up in poverty. It is a crime that we should allow such a unique and marvellous creature to starve to death, or to die in squalor in a slum. It is a crime that we should accept such things as racism, caste systems and bigotry when each individual on this planet is a wonder, whole and complete in him- or herself.

Christianity does not believe in human rights. It believes in superhuman rights. There are no mere humans, there are only immortals waiting for their chance to live for ever.

■ ■ ■ ■

When we forget that all humans are special, we can do with them what we will.

I once went to Dachau, site of a notorious German concentration camp. What is truly shocking about Dachau is not just the death chambers and the harrowing statistics of killing and brutality, but its nearness. Unlike so many Nazi death camps, put on the outskirts of the empire, Dachau is right in the heart of Germany, only a 15-minute train journey from Munich.

The camp has been preserved, a chilling reminder of the way in which brutality is never far from the human heart. It is just a short journey away from us, for it begins with a simple denial. It begins with the words, 'You are not the same as me. You are different.'

Everything we do in life stems from how we view our fellow human beings. To reduce them to a series of chemical reactions, to believe that being a human is simply a matter of DNA and genetic codes, is to belittle humanity. It is one thing to remove a pile of chemicals, another thing entirely to kill a human being. Sacks of chemicals can easily be discarded; unique children of God cannot be ignored. If no one is special, then we are free to destroy on the basis of race, creed or colour; if all people have souls, then all must be saved and protected.

■ ■ ■ ■

What is true of humanity is also true of our world. If we are special, if we are created by God, then so is the world we walk on and all the creatures in it.

I remember a few years ago, sitting in a classroom and listening to a teenager passionately arguing that we should save the rhino from extinction.

'Why?' I asked.

He looked at me blankly. 'What do you mean, "why"?'

'What I say. Why should we save the rhino from extinction? What difference would it make?'

He looked even more blank. 'Because we should,' he ventured at last. 'Because it … it's the right thing to do.'

He was right, but he had not thought about it. It was clear that he – and his classmates – had bought into the green values of preserving endangered species. What they had not thought about was *why* this should be important.

The most powerful philosophical force in biology and zoology is evolutionary theory. Indeed, the idea of the survival of the fittest has spilled into all areas of life, and the phrase is now applied to economics, politics and social science as much as to zoology.

I have never understood how you can be both an evolutionist and a conservationist. It seems to me that to be a conservationist means that you are implacably opposed to the idea of 'the survival of the fittest'. It means that you will strive day and night to preserve creatures on the brink of extinction, creatures who, it might be said, have been proven in evolutionary terms to be surplus to requirements.

The fact is, however, that we feel a sense of loss when other species are under threat, a sense that things are not as they should be, that some kind of natural order is being undermined. Why should this be? Perhaps we recognize that every creature – not just human beings – is 'fearfully and wonderfully made'. Perhaps we see in every creature a unique design, a wonderful craftsmanship, a glorious outpouring of creative power.

Maybe, just maybe, we are also aware that it is our stewardship that is failing. As I tried to explain earlier, we cannot be held to account for the state of the world unless there is someone to account to. We cannot be held responsible for the state of the world's flora and fauna unless someone gave us the responsibility in the first place.

If the rhino is just a freak of evolution, if it is just a creature that has outlived its purpose, a product of some hidden force of nature, then there is no logical reason why I should feel remotely interested in its future. To put it bluntly: easy come, easy go. If, however, it is a creature of wonder and majesty, if it is an example of the glorious creativity of God, if it is part of my job to preserve these walking miracles, then I must fight with all my strength to preserve it.

If the rhino evolved by chance, then we should feel no compunction about letting it disappear. If it is part of the divine order, then it is up to all of us to preserve it, so that future generations can share in its majesty, mystery and might.

■ ■ ■ ■

The result of wonder is joy. Wonder is an exuberant emotion, an overflowing of delight in the world around us and the people who dwell on it. Yet we have become scared of joy, embarrassed by it. When the world around us is so grim and full of darkness, the joyful people are seen as the fools, the embarrassing ones.

This problem is exacerbated by certain cultures and nationalities. Being English, for example, means being constantly alert to the possibilities of embarrassment. We sense it instinctively. I can smell embarrassment at 25 yards.

That is one of the reasons why many people prefer religion to faith. Religion allows you to keep the proprieties. Religion is a dinner party where everyone dresses nicely and no one commits a faux pas. Religion is a matter of saying the right thing and meeting the right people.

I have never been much interested in religion. I would rather have joy. When we see the wonder of the world, we forget the proprieties. You cannot respond to wonder in a calm and measured way. Wonder demands that we respond with passion and delight, that we become like little children.

Personally, I feel this most when I pass a tree. There is something in me that still thinks trees are wonderful – so wonderful that I want to climb them. Normally I suppress the urge. I am nearly 40 years old. I have a house and a mortgage. Sometimes I even feel as if I have a proper job. Someone in my situation should not be climbing trees.

Oh, to hell with it! (I mean that literally.) Chuck away those shackles and get climbing. To hold back our natural delight in creation is a sin; to refuse to be like a child is to reject the thrill of living in God's world.

Throw your head back and laugh. Feel the thrill of it all! What a world we lose when we grow up!

■ ■ ■ ■

When we look at the world with wonder, we begin to ask questions. We begin to appreciate the marvel that we walk upon every day.

One of the things that children do is to ask questions. Lots of questions. Lots and lots of questions. That is their way of exploring, their way of working out what is going on. If the questions make no sense sometimes, what does that matter? They are not embarrassed by these questions. They are not afraid of looking stupid. They know only that there are many things to be discovered, and the only way to find out is to ask.

Too many Christians – and, indeed, too many followers of any faith – are too embarrassed or scared to ask questions. We think that asking questions implies a lack of faith. The Bible, however, is full of questions.

'Why did you do this?'

'Why do good people suffer?'

'Where are you?'

None of these questions is seen as an impertinence or a blasphemy. When the writer of a psalm cries to God, 'Where are you?' he does not assume that God has left for ever. He is asking a fundamental question about human experience. He is asking his father to explain.

The danger is not in the asking, but in our attitude. Questions asked out of genuine concern and interest are good questions, but too often we are like interviewers talking to politicians. Their aim is not to gain understanding, but to expose flaws. Their questioning is not exploration, but conquest. They are not interested in what the other person thinks, but in whether he or she can be made to look unthinking.

We make two mistakes. One is not to ask the questions of God, because we think that this is somehow showing disloyalty. Questions must be asked, however. Locked-in questions do not go away. They knock at the door of our prison; they hammer away. If we do not let them out, then we run the risk that their hammering will chisel through the foundations, bringing the whole building crashing to the ground.

The other mistake is to ask questions without wanting the answers. We interrogate God, but refuse to spend time listening to his answers. We fire our questions at God with the aim of breaking him down, forcing him to confess, leading him to his inevitable execution.

Question God, by all means. Ask what you will. But be prepared to listen. The answers might surprise you.

■ ■ ■ ■

To ask questions is to explore. Exploration is really the physical manifestation of wonder. It is wonder given direction. All exploration assumes that there are wonders to be seen and marvels to be discovered.

God is the last great continent. God is a land with no end, a sea with no shores. God is teeming with wonders and adventures.

■ ■ ■ ■

The world is more mysterious and strange than we can imagine. The real mysteries, however, are not 'X-Files'. They have nothing to do with monsters and aliens and Elvis appearing in a shopping mall.

The real mysteries are the pattern of water on a spider's web, the rebirth of plants in spring, the spirals of frost on a window, the silver flash of fish in the sea, the laughter of children, the love of man and woman, the longing for beauty, the love of God.

■ ■ ■ ■

BLUE WONDER

- Recognizes the uniqueness of all humans…
- Acknowledges our shared parenthood…
- Revels in the wonder of creation…
- And starts to explore.

Before he knew it, before he could react or prepare, they plunged into dense rolling cloud, yellow and sulphurous and charged with thunder. The frost that had sparkled in the mountain air was now splintery ice, whirling in the darkness. The air was heavy and thick, boiling, about to erupt.

'What's happening?' asked the man, but the girl just shook her head.

The temperature fell lower and lower. It was so cold that even standing close to the roaring burner he could feel no heat. His feet were numb, his nose was running and his head began to throb. The wind was picking up and across in the other corner of the basket, the girl was standing very still. There was a strange, muffled silence. It was not peace, but the terrible silence of unanswered cries.

'Are you all right?' she asked him.

'I'm fine,' he lied. Although cold, miserable and increasingly scared, he was not about to admit it to a little girl. 'Don't worry about me. It's all part of the adventure!' A sudden gust of wind whipped his cheeks and stung his eyes.

Still it grew colder and darker. Still the balloon ploughed on. Was it his imagination, or were they actually rising into the storm? It certainly seemed that the wind, which had guided them so gently, was now punishing them, attacking them and spinning them around, pushing them into the maelstrom.

Then the rain started to fall, icy cold and stinging. He tried to shelter under the canopy of the balloon, but the wind was so strong that the rain was blown in anyway.

Soon it was too much for him to bear. 'Don't you think we ought to take cover or something?' he shouted at last.

'Why?'

'Because it's raining! And it's getting very dark.'

'I keep telling you, this is a balloon. You can't fly against the wind. We can't turn back.'

'I don't want to turn back,' he lied again. 'I just wondered if there was a way around or something.'

'No,' she said sadly. 'There's no way round. We could descend and try to land...' She paused. 'But even then the storm would hit us. There's no avoiding it. There never is.'

'It's not that I want to land, really,' he said. 'It's just...' He hesitated.

'Yes?'

'Well, look at me! I'm soaking wet! I'm freezing!'

She threw her head back and laughed. It was a wonderful sound. It was a challenge thrown against the darkness.

'Why didn't you say so?' she said.

'I was trying not to bother you,' he said stiffly. 'I was trying to keep my end up. You know, act a bit heroic.'

She laughed. 'Honesty is true heroism,' she said. 'Here. I have some blankets.'

She pulled out a woollen blanket from the box on which she was sitting. Gratefully he caught it and *wrapped it about him.*

'You might have given me this earlier,' he grumbled.

'But you said you weren't cold.'

'Yes, but I was lying. I was just trying to be helpful.'

'It's more trouble to me that you weren't honest in your answers,' she said. 'In fact, it was more trouble to both of us. It's not easy getting blankets out in the middle of a storm.'

He wrapped the blanket more tightly about him and pulled it over his head. He peered gloomily into the darkness. The cloud was getting thicker and darker, and it seemed to the man that the swirling vapour was like walls closing in on him.

Now the storm really took hold of the balloon, tossing it like a seed on the air. In the distance a huge lightning flash crashed against the mountain, sending shards of rock cascading into the depths.

He gripped the side of the basket, but it was no use. He could feel the panic coming – that terrifyingly familiar feeling, the feeling he always had in tight spaces, the fear that he was being buried alive. He began to get short of breath. He was entombed by the cloud, so thick that he could not see across the basket. A thick, foggy cloud, dense with rain, descended on them, and suddenly he could no longer see beyond the end of his arm. He could hear the burner splutter and hiss, but could barely make out the red flame. What if it went out? What if disaster struck? Doubts pummelled him. What if the girl was no longer there?

What if she had been caught up and swept away by the wind? What if he was all alone, floating aimlessly towards the mountains? He had no idea how to steer this thing, how to land it, what to do…

'Where … where are you?' he cried at last. 'I can't see you!' No dignity now. No heroism left.

Now he was close to losing control. He began to sweat and shake. A blackness covered his eyes.

Just as he was going under, a hand caught him and held him tight.

'Don't worry,' said the girl. 'Hold my hand. I've got you.'

He felt an enormous sense of reassurance pass through him. He was still afraid, for the cloud was very thick, but it was enough just to know that someone else was there, just to feel that supporting hand. It was strange, to be sure, how the hand grabbing his was so strong, especially when he remembered the smallness of the girl who was piloting the balloon. He remembered how large her gloves were, but her hands were not gloved now. They were smooth and safe, and he thought of his mother. He said nothing. There would be time for questions later.

The rain stopped, but still the fog stayed there and the darkness was as thick as mud.

'We must keep going,' said the girl.

'I … I know,' he replied. 'It was just, you know – not knowing if anyone was there. I felt … lonely. Stupid of me in such a small balloon.'

Out of the gloom came her voice. 'It's not the space

between you, it's the space inside you. Even in the midst of a crowd we can be distant from each other.' She was close now. He could feel her warmth by his side. 'You can be terribly lonely in a crowd.'

'Will it be like this much longer?'

'I don't think so. No darkness lasts for ever. There will be an end. But as for this? Well, the journey always takes us through some darkness. No one ever travels completely in the light. Are you OK?'

'I'm OK. Let's continue with the journey.'

'This is the journey,' she added. 'Everything is the journey.'

'Where are we headed?'

'There's a valley ahead. Between the mountains. It won't be easy, but it's the only place to go. It's the only way to get out of this storm.'

'Very well. I think I can manage. As long as you're there. As long as I have someone to talk to.'

'Oh, you can always talk to me.' She laughed, and her laugh was like the first lifting of the cloud.

'Thank you,' he said. 'Let's keep going.'

friendship

In today's global, mobile world, we are starved of community. People are increasingly isolated, closed in their own worlds. In the comfort and safety of our own rooms we create a parody of communal life. We drink draught lager in a can so that we do not have to go to the pub; we watch movies on our home cinema system so that we do not have to go to the cinema; we send e-mails so that we do not have to talk to people; we enjoy a takeaway to avoid going to a restaurant; we watch the football on satellite TV to avoid going to a match.

These activities are not wrong in themselves, but they are not replacements for community. They are indications that we have forgotten how to share, or maybe that we no longer see the need for it. After all, everyone has disposable income these days. This is the gilt world. What we want, we go out and buy.

We have become insulated, remote and safe, dwellers in our own, private, well-oxygenated tent. Everything is close to hand. We have all that we need. We can keep free from interference, free from disease, damage and hurt. Free, in fact, from life.

But if there is no one to interfere, no one to intrude on us, then there is also no one to care. If there is no one walking with us, then who will pick us up when we fall? Who will listen to our fears and hopes, our dreams and delusions? Who will be our friend?

■ ■ ■ ■

Friendship is a blue value. It is a fundamental of human existence, as basic to our lives as oxygen. Yet increasingly we are trivializing it, replacing it with superficial and spurious alternatives – the TV, the video game, the computer.

Friendship is a forgotten art. It has been sold off, privatized. The papers are full of adverts for chatlines and telephone sex. If we can find no true intimacy, we will pay someone else to listen to us or love us. Where once we spoke to friends and family, now we pay counsellors and therapists. Where once we were part of an extended family, now we have the welfare state. These undoubtedly good things are no replacement for the sense of belonging and community found in true friendship.

We need to cherish friendship. There are billions of people in the world – and so few friends.

■ ■ ■ ■

There are some pictures of flooding in a magazine. Massive deforestation high in the mountains has led to floods in the valley. With no trees to check the flow and hold the water under the soil, the rainwater has rushed too fast down the mountain slopes, carrying the soil away, swelling the rivers until, many miles downstream, the plains are flooded and hundreds and thousands of people are lost.

It is the roots which hold the world together. The trees staple the earth in place, gripping deep, holding the soil down, stopping the world from simply being washed away. Frost may damage a tree, storms may blast it, forest fire may scorch the branches, but the roots hold firm and the valley is safe.

Friendship, love, tradition, belonging: these are the things that root us, that keep us fixed and secure in our world. Take away those values, and what will happen when the floods come? What is there to hold us fast, to stop us from being washed away?

This sense of fragility, of living on the edge, is very strong today. The papers are full of talk about the disintegration of society, the collapse of the family. It is as if we can see the cracks appearing all around us, as if we can feel the flood waters rising.

We are constantly cutting down the trees in our lives. People are rootless; everything is always changing. We work in large, faceless corporations who do not care if we belong as long as we produce. We move cities, change jobs, forsake religion, leave our partners – and then wonder why we feel so lost.

The ground is shifting. The soil is moving beneath our feet. Battered by the winds of modern-day life, friendship is collapsing. It used to be about 'us', but now, like so much of the world around us, it is increasingly about 'me'. We are all on our own and when the wind blows and the rains come, we will all be swept into oblivion.

■ ■ ■ ■

How has this come about? Mainly because we have bought into the gilt value of treating everybody and everything as a product.

The sheer wealth of choice and the emphasis on the unbridled joy of the free market breeds a kind of consumer attitude to life. We are no longer citizens, but customers. Our only obligation is to pay, at the discount rate if possible. We are consumers of relationships, of values, of faiths. We consume in every sense: we select them, devour them, and then move on to the next. Choose the one to suit you, and if it shrinks, or if you do not like it, no problem! Buy another one. There are always thousands to choose from, all at low, low prices. After all, we do not want to pay too much for our friends, do we? And no one fixes anything any more. Trade it in and get a new one.

Members of the gilt generation do not value commitment. More than that, they are scared of it. It has become a taboo word. If we commit to something, what happens if we do not like it? It is safer to remain as we are, a nation of permanent browsers, 'just looking' at relationships, but never leaving the shop. In our mean world we have become miserly with the one currency that really matters: love. We hoard it up and stash it away. We will not risk it on what might not be a good investment.

So we start to look at people for what we can get out of them. As long as the relationship is serving my needs, then I will persevere, but the minute it gets difficult...

Friendships are not service contracts. We do not remain friends with people for what we can get out of them – at least, not if we want to keep our friends for long. We look for what is good for them, for what we can add. We look for how we can grow together.

■ ■ ■ ■

This is what I saw, all those years ago. I saw it with my own eyes, and when I close them I can still see it, just as clearly.

It happened because my master had let out a room for the festival, a room at the top of the house, and he'd sent me up to clear away the things. At that time there was this teacher and his friends in the city. They entered the city to all kinds of acclaim – people cheering and so on – but, like all these heroes, the whole thing ended in a mess. Of course, I've heard the rumours ever since. Some days I wonder if there's anything in them.

Anyway, they'd just finished the food and I was just starting to clear things away, when the teacher suddenly got up and took off his tunic. His friends looked at each other, with the kind of look that says, 'Here we go again.' I suppose they were used to it by then. After all, he was always doing something strange. That man lived to shock people.

He took a towel, wrapped it around his waist and slowly poured some water into a large basin. Then, starting at one end of the table, he knelt in front of each of his friends and washed their feet, washed away all the dust and the dirt, before drying them with the towel that was wrapped around him.

Then he reached this one man – huge, built like the coliseum. The man looked, I don't know, horrified. 'No,' he said. 'No, you can't do this. You're my Lord, not my servant.'

The teacher smiled at him and said, 'Look, just give in. Don't try to understand at the moment. Later it will all be clear.'

'I'm telling you, you shall never wash my feet,' said the huge man.

The teacher replied, 'But if I don't wash you, you have no part in me.'

For a moment there was one of those silences. You could tell the big man was thinking it through. Then he threw back his head and shouted, 'Then, Lord, you'd better wash the whole lot of me! Head, hands, feet – everything!'

Everyone laughed, especially the teacher. I wanted to stop and see what happened after that, but I had to go because my boss was calling me from outside. I've never forgotten that scene, though. Everything was the wrong way round – the teacher serving his pupils, the master washing his servants. It was as if I'd seen some great picture or statue. I've spent years thinking about it. Years.

What I remember most is wishing that someone would do that for me. I mean, that's what everyone wants, isn't it? Someone to wash them, someone to make them clean?

■ ■ ■ ■

There are houses in our cities that look like fortresses, apartments which look like cells. The windows are barred, the steel doors bolted. The poor, scared residents have been burgled so many times that the only solution they can think of is to imprison themselves.

I have met people who live barricaded lives, locked up in prisons of their own making. Scarred by their failed relationships, hurt by the wounds of betrayal and mistrust, they are no longer sure of anyone. They are always holding something back, something they can keep for themselves, just in case the betrayal happens once more. To protect their houses, they nail up the door. It keeps the intruders out, but unfortunately no one else can get in either.

■ ■ ■ ■

I watched a TV programme recently about the friendship between two rough sleepers. There, in a world where no one trusts anyone, they had found true friendship. 'I know that at night, when we cuddle close together for warmth, he won't rape me,' said one. Is that not what we all want? Someone who will give us warmth and love, but who will never abuse that trust? Too many people look for love and only get rape.

To trust is to make ourselves vulnerable, and to allow others to see our vulnerability. To trust is to unlock the doors and run the risk that someone will steal our hearts.

■■■■

Friendship is a blue value because it is the only way in which we can obtain the strength to do what must be done. It is only in friendship that we find support for our search – indeed, it means we can search together. Deep friendships arrive through deep conversations, through being honest with each other, through sharing more than just the superficial aspects of our lives.

Time is required for this. I was sitting on the train yesterday, working on my palmtop computer, listening to my minidisc player, consulting my pocket diary. Miniaturization is the buzz word. Everything is made smaller, more compact. We cannot miniaturize friendship. We must allow it to go in the opposite direction instead – to bloom and grow until it fills our houses and our lives. We must feed it with time and care, with attention and honesty.

Honesty is the most important thing of all. I have

friends who will ask me the tough questions, who will tell me when I am being an idiot – and because I know they care for me, because I trust them, I will listen to them.

With friends, when you ask, 'How are you?' you have to mean it.

■ ■ ■ ■

It has become fashionable to knock the family, to deny its strength. Despite all the statistics, despite all the evidence, cynics decry it as an outmoded institution, unnecessary in the modern world, a relic from an archaic age.

It is true that families can be damaging places, but they can also be places of great strength and comfort. When families are built around a core of honesty, forgiveness, acceptance, encouragement and love, they are the strongest and richest friendships the world has to offer.

A family filled with love will be a family filled with friends. It will be a family that is not competitive but complementary; where there is no pecking order or self-importance, only the awareness of what it means to be together.

Families – good families – have their traditions and little rituals, ways of binding themselves together and expressing shared values, shared experiences and affectionate humour. Such tradition and ritual can give us pattern and stability, but tradition and ritual only work if they are rooted in love. Commemoration becomes meaningless if no one really cares. A family is not a close-knit family just because everybody gathers round the same table every night. What builds closeness is not the presence of food and drink, but love and affection.

■ ■ ■ ■

London's Millennium Dome exhibition, I am told, will only be open for one year, and the building was only designed to last 25 years. It all seems so futile, so temporary. Yet that is standard in today's gilt world: build it big and impressive, throw money at it, but never forget – nothing is built to last.

It reminds me of a conversation I once had about marriage. 'No one expects it to last,' said a man to me. 'I mean, if it gets to 15 years, you've done well.'

We are creating marriages with built-in obsolescence – 'Dome-like' relationships characterized by a spectacular opening, a disappointing first year, then an unsettled existence while we try to work out what it is all for, before we tear it all down in a few years' time.

This is an inherently unhuman way of operating. Humans crave permanence. We want things to last. It is only lately that we have bought into the gilt values of rapidity and change. Gilt values say, 'Don't worry about the future – we have a bigger and better model coming along soon.'

Previous ages were not fooled by this approach. They built to last, knowing that great buildings do not come about overnight. They understood that their palaces and cathedrals, their villages and towns, would develop over the years, adapting themselves to the changing times, providing shelter and warmth and permanence.

Once again, fidelity is the key – the keeping of promises, the keeping of faith with each other. When we commit ourselves to our friends, our families, our partners, we do not do so in the naive belief that nothing will ever go wrong. Precisely the opposite is true. If everything was always going to run smoothly, there would be no need for commitment.

Commitment is a statement that, when things go wrong, I will still be there. When things are difficult and demanding, I will meet those difficulties and demands head on. I will not turn off the lights, lock the door and creep away to another house.

Marriage, ideally, is the deepest friendship, when two friends are so close that they have given everything to one another. In the Bible, Paul urges husbands to love their wives just as Christ loved us. How did Christ love those he met? He washed their feet, wept for them, healed them, reassured them and transformed them. He gave his life for them, reached down and pulled them from the grave.

Marriage is a kind of resurrection. Each person 'dies' for the other, killing what they want for themselves, killing their own selfish desires, in order to seek what is best for their partner. In doing so, each of them receives new life.

It demands of us that we listen, love, talk, share, encourage, learn every day. In marriage we should demand the best for each other – a best that can only be achieved through mutual sacrifice and love.

■ ■ ■ ■

In Fiji, apparently, it is taboo to touch someone's hair – as bad as it would be to touch the genitals of someone in our own Western culture. In Thailand, the top of a girl's head is a no-go area. In Japan you may not touch the nape of a girl's neck. All cultures have certain parts of the body which it is forbidden to touch.

In marriage, however, these taboo areas do not apply. Marriage is a willing acceptance of profound intimacy. It is the place where we allow another person to reach out to every part of our lives – even those areas of our being that are 'off limits' to everyone else.

There are areas of our life that we do not want to talk about, that we wish to hide away. We put up the warning signs – 'Do Not Touch' – but in marriage we grant permission for touching, not only physically, but also spiritually and emotionally.

That is why the intimacy of lovers is not to be entered into lightly or without promise and trust. Physical intimacy, on its own, carves off one part of the whole. The physical expression of marriage is a sign, a symbol, of the entire relationship. Without the other part of the relationship, without trust and true love, it will always be fundamentally empty, a symbol devoid of true meaning.

Physical intimacy without emotional and spiritual intimacy is damaging and confusing. We risk opening ourselves to someone who does not really care and who is not really committed to us as a person. We are more delicate creatures than we appear, and we need careful treatment – as the shop sign says, 'Fragile – Handle With Care'. There are so many people who have been picked up and dropped, smashed on the floor, betrayed by a false understanding of what it means to love and be loved.

Gilt values say that sex is meaningless, a mere physical activity, as innocuous as a game of tennis or a jog in the park. Yet there will inevitably be consequences every time intimacy is cheapened and love devalued. There is a deadening of the soul, a cancerous growth of mistrust and bitterness. Cheap sex has cheapened sex. It has led to an immature society, unable to outgrow casual relationships and meaningless intimacy.

Another shop sign reads, 'All Breakages Must Be Paid For'. There are many people who have allowed others to reach a level of intimacy with them, but whose trust has been cruelly abused and betrayed. Sometimes they really loved the other person; more often they were just following the false sexual norms of our culture.

What about those who are not married? Are they to be denied this intimacy? What about those who have been hurt? What about those who have been betrayed? Are they to be forever denied the freedom of intimacy?

Not at all, for there is another person in all cultures who is free of the restrictions of taboo. In every culture, when a mother cares for her child, no area is hidden, no element is taboo. God is both father and mother, and nothing is hidden from him, no area of our life is too shocking or too outrageous, no pain too hidden, no secret too taboo.

This is difficult. Being human, we crave physical affection and the love that it signifies. Yet we must believe that God loves us – that he hugs us, like the old man in the story, welcoming back his lost son.

Sometimes in the lonely nights, it may feel as if we have been exiled from the world of physical comfort, as if we are living in another country, in a dark, nightmare world. It is at that moment that our Father can come to us, mother-like in his love. One of the psalms in the Bible tells us that God holds our hand, like a parent holding the hand of the child he knows so well:

If I rise on the wings of the dawn,
if I settle on the far side of the sea,
even there your hand will guide me,
your right hand will hold me fast.

If I say, 'Surely the darkness will hide me
and the light become night around me,'
even the darkness will not be dark to you;
the night will shine like the day,
for darkness is as light to you.
For you created my inmost being;
you knit me together in my mother's womb.

Psalm 139

God holds our hand. Or he kneels before us and washes our feet. Tender, caring, like a mother washing a baby.

■ ■ ■ ■

Friendship is a sacrament – a visible sign of what God is like. In true friendship we talk, listen and love. We love unconditionally, but not uncritically. We forgive, build up, encourage, comfort and enjoy. We behave, in short, like God.

■ ■ ■ ■

Friendship is expressed in the hands and arms. It can be a hand pulling someone from danger, an arm across the shoulder, hands clasped in greeting, a warm embrace, a stroll through the park, arm in arm. Sometimes it can be a slap in the face.

'Opposition is true friendship,' wrote William Blake, a man who, if this statement is correct, had a lot of friends. He identified a deep truth nonetheless: true friendship means confrontation as well as consolation. If I love someone, if I care for them, then I will not stand aside and let them damage others or themselves. Even if it means risking the friendship, there will be a time when I need to step in and shake them. There will also be a time when they need to do the same to me.

■ ■ ■ ■

In the old children's story *The Velveteen Rabbit*, the toy Rabbit asks his friend the Skin Horse what 'real' is.

'Real isn't how you are made,' says the Skin Horse. 'It's a thing that happens to you. When a child loves you for a long, long time, not just to play with, but REALLY loves you, then you become Real.'

We are not 'real' just because we are flesh and bone. We do not 'belong' just because we have been placed on this planet. We are made real by love and we belong when others care. We are made real by the love in the hearts of our friends and family, by the love in the heart of God.

We are real, not because we are made of matter, but because we matter. When other people care about us, then we become significant, then we start to belong, then we are made Real.

■ ■ ■ ■

It is only by loving that we can learn how to love. It is only by trusting that we can learn how to trust. Friendship is the practical expression of love. Through faithfulness, through trust, through a deep commitment to sharing our lives with others, we provide a place where people can learn about God.

People are yearning for somewhere where they can belong. In this rootless, ever-changing, shifting world, they are looking for a place they can call home.

This place will not be a geographical location. You can feel lonely and lost in your own bed. Belonging is not linked to a physical place, but to a group of people, to the hearts and lives of others.

Where our friends are, there we belong – and, because we take our friendship with us, we know that we will always belong. Our belonging is not rooted in one place, but in each friendship.

What is the commonest expression of loneliness? 'I don't matter. Nobody cares about me.'

God cares – always. Our real friends care – and through them we see the face of God.

■ ■ ■ ■

BLUE FRIENDSHIP

- Enjoys honest, open, deep conversations…
- Offers commitment and security…
- Preserves the sanctity of intimacy…
- And roots society through love.

Gradually the mists cleared. The air was dark with the shadow of night, but beyond the mountains the sun had not yet completely set. Indeed, were it not for the brightness of the sun beyond the mountains, the world would have been unbearable.

He dropped the girl's hand, almost embarrassed to be seen holding it. She did not seem remotely concerned. Instead, she was peering ahead of her.

'Look!' she said, excitedly. 'That's where we're heading. Straight through there.'

He looked ahead. Straight ahead, rising almost vertically for thousands of feet, were two sheer walls of black granite. Their sides were almost smooth, the rock glistening with a veneer of ice. Between the cliffs was a thin, vertical line of yellow light, a perilously narrow gap between the two massive walls of rock.

The man stared in horror. 'You're joking!' he said. 'We can't get through that – we'll be smashed to pieces!'

'Well, what's your alternative?'

'Can't we go in a different direction?'

'I don't know how many more ways there are to say this,' she replied, 'but we're being blown by the wind. For the last time, this is not an aeroplane. We have to go in that direction.' She paused. 'Everyone has to go in that direction.'

'Well, take us up then. We can go over.'

'Have you seen how high these mountains are?'

He looked up. The cliffs soared into the sky, like two enormous tombstones. They stretched to the left and the right, filling the horizon with a solid wall of darkness as far as the eye could see. There was no way they were going to get over them. Their only hope was to head for the gap.

'Is there no other way?'

She shook her head. 'The cliffs are very strong,' she said, 'but very thin. It only takes a moment to go through.'

'I just hope you know what you're doing.'

'Have I ever let you down?'

'There's always a first time.' The girl turned and looked at him for a moment. A tremendous solemnity came over him, as if something very important was being said amongst the simple words. 'No,' he said at last. 'You haven't.'

'Good, then,' she smiled. 'Let's go for it.'

She pulled on the burner valve and the balloon rose. The cliffs were near now, sheer and black and forbidding. He knew instinctively that, if the balloon were to miss the pass, they would be doomed. There were no ledges, no outcrops, nowhere for the balloon to land. They would just smash into the sides of the cliff and slither down the vertical sheets of ice, squashed like bugs on a windscreen.

The cliffs were like two huge doors. At any moment he expected them to slide together, to close the gap, to shut him out for ever.

The man held his breath. The world seemed to hold still. There was no noise, except for the murmur of the wind, the flapping of rope on canvas and the occasional roar of the burner. Now black rock was all he could see, coming towards them like an enormous wave. Fifty yards to go. He thought of his house in the valley. How could he have wanted to leave it for this foolish adventure? Forty yards. Yet this adventure was, he knew, the turning point of his life. Thirty yards. It was nothing like he had imagined it to be, but it was more than he had ever hoped for. Twenty yards. But to lose his life ... what could be gained by that? Ten yards...

Then he knew what was to be gained. He saw the light streaming through the gap and, just for a moment, he thought he saw fields and sunlight and water. Then, suddenly, he knew the journey was worth it. He felt an immense surge of gratitude towards this girl, this little creature who had helped him to fly. Whatever happened, he knew that he had been loved, taught, changed and made joyful – and nothing else mattered.

'I just wanted to say...' he began. But there was no time. The wind pushed them through and suddenly they were a part of the mountain. For a moment, for the briefest moment, they were surrounded by blackness and everywhere was rock and the universe was hard, cold stone, but then they were through and out the other side.

She was right. The door to the valley was as thin as skin. Suddenly all was light and colour and warmth. A valley was spread out before them, appearing from the darkness as if by magic, a valley overflowing with sunlight and filled with grass, trees, water and birds, *singing in the warm air. He had thought the sun was setting, but it had merely been hidden by the dark stone. For a moment the cliffs had blotted out the sun, but on this side, he knew that the sun would shine for ever.*

'We made it!' he shouted. 'We did it!'

'Told you,' said the girl.

'Where are we?'

The valley shimmered in the heat. Fields rippled gently in the wind. Meadows rich with colourful flowers ran down to a lake of the purest blue.

'We're at the landing site,' said the girl. 'Time to take us down.' She turned to him and smiled. 'It must be nice to be on familiar territory.'

'But I don't know this place,' said the man. 'I've never been here before.'

'Are you sure?'

Then he realized that some of it did look familiar. The place seemed to be filled with echoes of the world he had left – or was it the other way round? Had it really been that the beauty of the old world was merely a dim reflection of this valley?

They coasted down, following the course of the valley, and skirted over the top of a small wood until they spotted a large clearing below them. In the clearing stood a little house. The man looked at it. Something about it looked very familiar.

'I sort of recognize that...' he murmured. 'Maybe I have been here before after all.'

She pulled on a thin piece of rope and the balloon

began to descend, sliding down until finally it came to rest with the lightest of bumps on the soft grass. They were in the field by the house. In the middle of the field were two posts, both with large metal rings in them. Nimbly, the girl jumped out and tethered a large rope to one ring. Then she ran across to the other ring and did the same for the other side. The balloon was anchored, finally at rest.

Cautiously, the man climbed out of the basket. His legs were shaking, but whether with relief or excitement he could not say. He looked at the rings, holding the balloon.

'You've been here before,' he said to the girl.

'To this destination,' she said, 'but not to this place.'

'How can the place be different?'

'It just is. Every time. Each journey has a different destination, yet every destination is the same.'

The man sighed. 'Another paradox.'

The girl giggled. 'Well, what do you expect?' she said. 'They're such fun. Everywhere is different,' she continued dreamily, 'but everywhere is home.' Her gaze, which had been roaming over the valley, fixed itself on the little cottage. 'Look.'

The man looked towards the building, and then he realized: it was his house. It was the house he had left back in the town, somehow transported to this remote valley, halfway up a mountain on the other side of the world. It was his house as he remembered it: small, comforting, with everything he needed; a place without pretence, a place where he could be himself. And yet it was somehow different – more solid, more intense, more real.

'It's my house,' he said. 'Yet it seems, I don't know … brighter.'

'That's because you understand it more now. You know what it means.'

'Do I?'

'Oh yes. Things are always more solid when you know what they stand for.'

The man shook his head. 'I'll get used to it in time, I suppose,' he said, looking around. 'Nice neighbour-hood.'

'Hey!' shouted the girl. 'I've just remembered! Champagne!'

'What?'

'Champagne! Every balloon trip ends with your free, celebratory glass of champagne!' She rushed back to the balloon, leant over the basket, tipping her legs in the air whilst she rummaged in one of the lockers, and emerged with two glasses and a bottle.

She fumbled with the bottle. There was a pop and the champagne frothed into the two glasses.

'Here,' she said.

He looked deep into the glass. It was golden and sparkling and overflowing. It was his heart, his soul, his feelings, his life.

'Cheers,' he said.

'Bottoms up,' said the girl. She took a gulp and gig-gled. 'It's always the same,' she said. 'The bubbles get up my nose.'

'Should you be drinking this stuff?' said the man. 'Aren't you a bit young?'

She laughed. 'So it might appear,' she said.

He laughed and raised his glass again. 'A toast to you, my little pilot,' he said. 'Here's to all the adventures and all the lessons and, oh, the glorious danger of it all!' The light sparkled on the glass. 'Here's to all that's happened!'

'And all that will happen!' shouted the girl in high excitement.

'What do you mean?'

'Oh, my goodness,' she said. 'You don't think a journey like this ends, do you?'

'But I'm home,' he said. 'Sort of.'

'Exactly. And it will always be here. Everything will be the same and nothing will be the same. Everything is as you remember it, but nothing is what you expect. Every day will be an adventure and a challenge and a glass of champagne.'

'I'll drink to that.' He took a deep drink from the glass.

He started to walk towards the house, but then he turned. 'Do I have to go in yet?' he asked.

'Of course not.'

'Only, it's such a lovely day … and the sun's so bright … and the breeze is so gentle…'

'Yes?' The girl broke into a huge grin and it seemed as if her smile filled the valley.

'Well,' he said. 'Is there any chance of another flight?'

celebration

Human beings are celebratory animals. From the time of the cavemen, we have always turned to music around the fire, dancing, storytelling, feasting. These were celebrations – communal gatherings, filled with mystery and significance.

In our gilt-valued world we have lost that significance. Now every night is party night, every night is a riot of over-indulgence, every night is meaningless.

The laughter is hollow, the champagne flat. We are partying, but we have nothing to celebrate.

■ ■ ■ ■

Say what you like about human beings, but we really know how to have a good time. Admittedly, most of the time we do not know why we are having a good time, and sometimes we cannot remember what the good time was like, and sometimes the good time is followed by a really, really bad time…

'Eat, drink and be merry,' is our motto, 'for tomorrow we diet.' Tonight we will drink, dance and stuff ourselves silly – and if it all seems rather pointless, well, who cares?

I care. I care that we should learn the difference between parties and celebration. The difference will demonstrate whether there really is anything in our lives to get excited about.

There is indeed a difference between celebrating and partying. In the gilt world we have turned 'having a good time' into a mission statement. We are obsessive over-indulgers. In many countries alcohol consumption is enormous, especially among the 18–25 age group. The idea of a good time is to go out and get hammered, before falling asleep or throwing up.

Such revelry is characterized by escape. There are drugs to help you escape reality; one-night stands to help you escape commitment; drink to help you escape from pain; crowding together to disguise the loneliness and isolation. In Dr Johnson's words, people become beasts to 'escape the pain of being a man'.

People get out of their heads on alcohol, not because they feel important, but because they feel insignificant. It is precisely because they feel in their hearts that life is futile, that pleasure is fleeting, that they do not matter, that they drown such feelings with activity, alcohol and noise. To get out of control is the only real control they have in their lives.

The reality is that our celebration of significant events is marked by increasingly desperate attempts to escape our own feelings of insignificance. The escape can never be anything more than temporary. Come the morning, come the end of the party, the reality must be faced.

■ ■ ■ ■

I have been watching a TV programme about holiday-makers on a Greek island. These revellers, all young (or trying to be young), have two aims: to get drunk and to get laid. Perhaps they have to achieve one to endure the other.

It was unutterably sad to watch the relentless, aimless energy with which they battled the pointlessness of their lives. Their only goal is a momentary physical pleasure, a fragment of fake intimacy, a brief instant of self-absorbed satisfaction. They dance with desperation, they drink to forget the miserable boredom of their lives, they sleep with each other to disguise the fact that they are so very alone.

Joy without meaning is self-delusion, a song in the dark, a spasm, not a dance.

■ ■ ■ ■

Throughout our society we have lost the sense of meaning behind so many festivals and holidays. Public holidays are spent at the garden centre, or playing golf or football, or just in sleeping and recovering from the stresses of the rest of the week.

Holidays and festivals have their roots in religious celebration. They are not arbitrary dates, but dates chosen to plant the year with celebrations. Christmas – the birth of Christ – offers light and hope in the deep, dark winter. Easter – the resurrection of Christ – celebrates new life, the death of death.

We have divorced these events from their context. In the UK, for example, we no longer have church festivals but 'bank' holidays. Parties with God have turned into days when the banks do not open. Holy days have become vacations, a series of vacant days – empty, devoid of meaning.

■ ■ ■ ■

On TV last night there was a documentary about the brain, specifically about those parts of the brain which deal with memory. It featured a young boy whose memory was practically nonexistent. He could not remember family events, holidays, things that had happened to him in the past. He had trouble remembering names or faces.

What had happened to him was a specific kind of amnesia, one that meant he could not attach any emotional significance to events. Most of us remember certain times clearly because we associate them with strong emotions. I remember a great deal about my wedding day, for example, but I do not remember much about the day before or even the day after. They were not so emotionally significant.

This boy knew the facts about his past. He knew that he had celebrated birthdays and Christmases, that he had enjoyed days out and big events, but he could not attach emotional significance to them. Effectively, therefore, the past was a blank to him. It is a terrible disability. As I sat there, I tried to imagine what it would be like to have no cherished memories, no special moments to look back on.

This is precisely what is happening in our society today. We have the same kind of amnesia, the same inability to attach importance to things, the same lack of profound memories. We can remember the technique of celebration all right; we can put on the parties – but we have no memories to attach to the events. We have lost the ability to create significance. We dance on, our lives lost in grey insignificance.

■ ■ ■ ■

The motto of a party is, 'Eat, drink and be merry, for tomorrow we die.' The motto of a celebration is, 'Eat, drink and be merry, for today we have started to live.'

Celebration is different from partying. A celebration has significance and meaning. A celebration seeks to rejoice in life, not to escape into oblivion. Celebrations are joyful and they know the reason for their joy. A celebration is a party with hope, a dance at the point where past, present and future meet – where, living in the present, we give thanks for the past and look forward to the future.

If we are really to move forward into the blue, we have to relearn how to celebrate. More than that, we have to have something to celebrate in the first place.

At the heart of any celebration is a story. It might be the story of a life, of a year gone by, or of the love of two people. Wedding celebrations demonstrate this precisely. They celebrate a story, a tale of companionship and growth, a bond between two people that has fidelity and trust. As anniversaries go by, more chapters are added to the tale. It may be a simple story, a tale that is easily told, but it is a story all the same – an emotional high point, a meaningful celebration.

What is important is that we have a tale to tell. We need emotional high points and lives that are worth celebrating. Without this, celebration is impossible. An absence cannot be celebrated. It can only be mourned.

■ ■ ■ ■

In the Bible, in Luke's Gospel, there is a story about a man named Zacchaeus. Zacchaeus was that scariest of beings, a little man with a lot of power – an inferiority complex with clout. He was the man who collected the taxes, who set the rates, who – backed by the occupying forces – could effectively charge what he liked.

At least he knew that he was hated. He knew that he was an outcast and something in him realized that he did not want to be an outcast all his life. Gradually the alienation, the loneliness, built up inside him until he could take it no longer. He did the only thing he could.

He climbed a tree.

Zacchaeus climbed a tree to see Jesus as he

walked by. Just to see him was all he wanted, but Jesus stopped, looked up and invited himself to the tax-collector's house. From that moment Zacchaeus's life was changed.

Sometimes, making a fool of ourselves is the wisest course of action. If it means that God looks up and laughs, if it means that he looks into our eyes and invites himself into our house, then acting like a fool is the wisest thing to do.

That day, Zacchaeus held a real celebration, per-haps the first one ever. He knew he had found the sig-nificance he longed for, and he knew, perhaps, that significance is not measured in physical stature or wealth, or even in the ability to climb trees. It is mea-sured in who sits in our house and hosts the celebration.

■ ■ ■ ■

The Bible talks a lot about celebration, which may come as a surprise to those who think of it as a stern and dull book. I remember my shock at discovering that Jesus was heavily criticized for attending too many parties. They even accused him of being a drunkard.

Jesus' parties were messy – people drank wine, talked too loud and too embarrassingly, poured per-fume over other people's feet. He invited all those people who should not really go to parties, all those people who did not know how to behave.

Most of all, Jesus' parties were celebrations. They were all festivals, rejoicing in the great story of God come to earth. The story they were celebrating was the one about the homecoming, the one where the old man greets his son on the road, the one about the child returning to his father.

■ ■ ■ ■

Celebration is a blue value. It urges us to find what is meaningful in our life and make it the cause of our joy. It calls on us to remember the meaning behind the event, to live lives that are worth celebrating.

Perhaps it has more to do with an attitude. If, instead of the hope of escape, we were to take into those parties the love of our partner, the closeness of old friends, the wonder of the world, the friendship of God, then the party would be transformed. We would no longer be aimlessly over-indulging, but truly celebrating, dancing into the light, drinking in the joy of being alive.

■ ■ ■ ■

Yes. Celebration is not an event, but an attitude. It is the dance at the still point, the wondrous joy of the now, the ascent to the peak. On one side of the mountain is the past, on the other side is the future – but the peak of the mountain is the now, and it is good to spend time on the mountain top.

Rather than celebrate, therefore, we should aim to be celebrations: walking, talking reminders of what has been done for us and what is yet to come.

It is difficult to be a celebration. Often, I fear, I am more funeral than anything else – a tired, stressed-out writer, made irritable by the never-ending difficulty of finding the right words and writing them down. This is not what I want. I want to be something different. I want to be a joyful traveller, illuminated by truth and lit up by love.

Jesus threw parties. He also went to weddings. At one wedding in a place called Cana, urged on by his mother, he performed a miracle. He turned huge jars of dishwater into fine wine. It is a powerful image, for it mirrors what he has done for all those who follow him. Loved by God, we have been made special, we have been turned into wine.

What vintage, I wonder, has he turned me into? Am I *vin ordinaire*? Am I, perhaps, not the real thing at all – a fake, a cheap red with a false label pasted on? I do not want to be like that. I want to be something different. I want to be overflowing with joy and love, bubbling over with enthusiasm, hope, faith and wonder.

I want to be champagne.

■ ■ ■ ■

BLUE CELEBRATION

● Celebrates significance…
● Tells a story…
● Lives as a celebration…
● And dances in the light.

There was once a man who wanted to fly in a balloon. That was his dream and his ambition: to rise above the earth; to rise into the blue sky and leave the world behind him...

■ ■ ■ ■

Two men were walking back from the city. Their minds were confused, befuddled with conflicting news and reports. No one doubted that their friend had died. He had been killed by the authorities, who were known for their thoroughness in these matters. He had been buried. But now ... now people were claiming to have seen him again.

They wanted to find out the meaning of all this, and so they started walking.

As they trudged along, they were joined by a third man, a stranger. 'Why so sad?' he asked, looking at their downcast eyes, noticing the way they dragged their feet.

'Are you from another planet?' asked one of the men bitterly. 'Haven't you heard what's been happening in the city? Don't you know about the death?'

The stranger did not answer, so they went on to tell him everything. They told him how they had expected so much of their friend and how it had all come to nothing. Then they told him the latest stories – fantastic tales of how their friend had been seen alive. They shared with him their confusion and their hope. 'We don't know what to believe,' they said.

The stranger laughed. 'You know what your trouble is?' he said. 'You're looking down at the road. If you want answers, you have to look up.' He laughed again, as they looked so confused. 'Come on,' he said. 'I'll tell you a story. Now, heads up and listen!'

He began at the beginning and explained to them everything that they had wondered about. Being a stranger, his story was very strange and very wonderful, and it was as if their hearts were on fire.

They approached their destination and, for a moment, it looked as though the stranger was going further, as if he intended to walk all night.

'Stay,' they said. 'Come home with us. Have something to eat.'

So he went with them to their homes. There was bread on the table and the stranger picked it up and broke it.

Then they knew. They knew who he was and what it meant and why the strangeness was so strangely familiar. Above all, they knew that he would always be walking, hand in hand with all who walk the road of love.

■ ■ ■ ■

We are back where we started. People are looking for meaning. Some are slowly walking back home, some are searching junk shops, some are even climbing trees, just to get closer to the blue.

■ ■ ■ ■

Above all, do not lose the desire to walk: every day I walk myself into a state of wellbeing and walk away from every illness; I have walked myself into my best thoughts, and I know of no thought so burdensome that one cannot walk away from it... Thus, if one keeps on walking, everything will be all right.

Søren Kierkegaard

■ ■ ■ ■

My journey has been a search for values, values to give life meaning and hope. They are values because they are valuable. We should treasure them because they are treasures.

That does not mean we should lock them away. We must use them, make them part of our lives. They will grow richer and more real with use. They are not museum pieces or collector's items. They are not fragile or antique, these values, but strong and alive. The more we use them, the stronger and more alive we shall be.

They are not solely for our use either. They are gifts for ourselves and to pass on to others. The only thing to do with the truly valuable things in life is to give them away.

These values are the basis of a truly fulfilled life, but we must each walk the road for ourselves. There are treasures to be found, but it is up to each one of us to search for them.

■ ■ ■ ■

Hope, faith, stillness, truth, mercy, wonder, friendship, celebration.

And love.

Back at the beginning of the journey, love was on my list of values, on the itinerary of places to be visited. As I started to write, however, I became aware that love was not a place to be visited but the country through which we were to travel, the landscape surrounding us all. You cannot separate love from the other values, for it is fundamental to all of them. It is the road beneath our feet, the heaven over our heads. Love is the landscape of our lives.

If nothing else, this exercise in thinking has convinced me of one thing. My story, like everyone else's, is fundamentally about love. It is about the love of an old man for his son; the love of an innocent man for his killers; the love of a traveller for the journey. It is a long story, a twisting story, a story with pain and pleasure, hope and fear, joy, laughter, sadness and surprise.

It is a story with a beginning, a middle and no end. I cannot see how the plot will twist and turn. I cannot see what heights I have to scale and what depths I have to descend.

I do know who will be with me as I walk.

■ ■ ■ ■

Walk the road by yourself and you will only wander. Walk with God and you will go home.

■ ■ ■ ■

I cannot sleep tonight. Instead I get out of bed and look through the window. The night is dark. The stars are shining. I am thinking about the journey. And the sky – the sky is blue.